I Just Want to

Pee Alone

a collection of humorous essays by

Kick Ass Mom Bloggers

@throat_punch Books

Copyright 2013 by @throat_punch Books

All rights reserved.

This book is dedicated to every mother who dreams of

peeing alone.

TABLE OF CONTENTS

I Just Want to

Pee Alone

INTRODUCTION

Motherhood is tough enough, especially if you can't laugh at the rogue hairs on your chin or when you didn't realize your child accidentally used your toothbrush until after you were done brushing your teeth with it too.

I've always said I need a village to help me raise my children. I just have one stipulation: if you're going to be in my village, then you'd better have a terrific sense of humor. You can't take yourself too seriously if you're going to help me parent my kids, because I sure don't.

I don't know about you, but I'm always looking to surround myself with other funny moms, because motherhood is a serious business. You're raising little people here. You're molding the future leaders of the world. But you know what? You're also doing something that women have done for centuries. Sure, you *could* be raising a future President of the United States, but you could also be raising a future shift manager of Taco Bell, so easy there. Raising kids is tough and you might as well laugh, or else you're going to cry.

I love my kids. Don't we all? But do you know what else I love? I also love all-day Kindergarten and early bedtimes. I love Moms' Night Out and Date Night with the Hubs. But I especially love anything that gives me five minutes of uninterrupted peace to myself to JUST PEE ALONE!

A year ago I felt like I was the only funny mom on the block. I couldn't find another mom who thought it was hilarious when my daughter asked me why my "china has a mustache" or when my son thought I was older than my mother. Luckily, I didn't have to look too far. I found a terrific group of hysterical and hilarious women on the internet.

I've put together a book full of my favorite bloggers and I'm so excited to share them with you. All of these bloggers have such a unique and humorous look at motherhood and I know you'll find a story in here that will resonate with you and make you laugh out loud.

Jen of People I Want to Punch in the Throat

The Naked Starfish
By Kim Bongiorno
Let Me Start By Saying

When I was a spritely, single 20-something working in New York City, I never hesitated to pamper myself.

A sexy satchel would wink at me from a store window: I'd pop in and buy it.

Sunday afternoons were spent giving myself homemade facials and sparkly pedicures.

I worked hard, and made a point to hunt down the pampering I deserved.

From the moment I was first pregnant, and those around me insisted that treats such as cold cuts and nail polish could cut my unborn child's potential IQ in half, I got into the habit of *not* seeking out the little things that brought me joy. Like soft cheese. And getting too close to a Starbucks.

Then my son came, and I was too busy crying while searching for his User Manual to consider a manicure or a massage.

I lasted about a week as a new mom before reaching out to others in my situation online. As exhausted, cranky, and confused as I was, I needed friends.

It didn't take long for this gaggle of desperate, sleepless women to meet up in person. A handful of us clicked like old friends from the start, and we decided to celebrate making it to our kids' first birthdays with a Moms' Weekend at the spa.

The concept of an entire weekend away seemed crazy. Selfish.

I Just Want to Pee Alone

Totally. Awesome.

We had our bags packed a month ahead of time.

In October of 2006, five of us headed out on our kidless adventure. It was the first time any of us had spent a night away from our families since we became parents. For two of us (including me), it was the first and last time we'd get away for a while, since we had already managed to get ourselves knocked up again.

I was about twelve weeks into a pretty tough pregnancy, but refused to cancel my plans. I had booked a body wrap for Saturday morning, and prayed I'd feel well enough to go through with it. I knew I deserved to relax, but also knew it would take me a week to recover from the effort. Honestly, that weekend would have been considered a success if all that had happened was that we each got two days of uninterrupted bowel movements, but we had a lot of lost pampering time to make up for.

Why is it that when you try to do nice things for yourself once you're a parent, it always feels like a compromise?

None of us were in the habit of pampering ourselves anymore. Heck, none of us were in the habit of showering regularly anymore, but we were determined to fight the good fight and make the most of every minute of this vacation from reality.

We stumbled into our quiet suites and began a weekend of trying to figure out how to relax and enjoy ourselves while wrapped in the threads of Mom Guilt that had secretly wound around us over the past year.

I woke up the next morning wanting to stay in bed, but insisted on soaking up every luxury I could, even if it killed me, so we all-headed over to the spa facilities.

I stripped down to my birthday suit in the spa bathroom like the desk clerk told me to do for the wrap, quickly covering up with a fluffy robe, as my less-uptight friends changed in the main locker area. Holding the robe tight, so as to not accidentally flash anyone, I blushed furiously at the thought of someone getting a peek of my private parts due to an overzealous leg crossing or too-loose belt knot.

With all the poking and prodding I had during my pregnancies, you'd think my prudishness about public nudity would have waned. *Not the case.* I was still the girl who didn't wear shorts unless it was over a hundred degrees out. I was still the girl who hadn't owned a skirt in fifteen years. I was uncomfortable even with this naked-under-my-robe situation, but fought through it in the name of relaxation.

Because nothing's more relaxing than battling the threat of a wardrobe malfunction.

Everyone else comfortably chatted as hints of their cleavage peeked out, and bathrobe hemlines slid up their bare thighs. I averted my eyes, and held on tight until my name was called.

When we entered my treatment room, table prepped to discreetly wrap me up like a burrito, the lady who was to do my wrap stopped short and said, "I'm sorry, but we can't do wraps on pregnant women."

I told her that I had confirmed they could with four of their employees, so she went out to grab her manager, who came to tell me that they absolutely could not do it. I asked for a pregnancy massage instead, but they said the only other treatment room available at that time was a body scrub.

I wanted a wrap. I'd settle for a massage. If I were home, I'd cancel the appointment and wait for exactly what I wanted. Actually, if I were home I'd be elbow-deep in someone else's poop, so I bucked up and accepted the offer of a body scrub. I used to like to try new things, and, really, how bad could it be?

We walked into the adjoining room, and what stood before me looked like a waterboarding platform for starfish.

The treatment room was giant and glaringly white. It had a massive chrome rod with seven showerheads hanging from the ceiling, and the floor was made of NYC subway tiles. It was like walking into a kinky couples' resort's shower stall, but without the romance, and with some random lady I had met only seven minutes earlier.

There was no changing area. There was no privacy screen.

As casually as she could manage, and without meeting my eye, the therapist told me to remove my robe and lay down on the table.

Totally naked. On the starfish table.

Let's take stock. Yes, I wanted to have this luxurious spa treatment done. No, I didn't want this woman seeing my bits and pieces.

I believe this is what one calls "a dilemma."

I had to force myself to be reasonable. *She sees naked people all the time. You're just another body she has to work on, like she's a bored mechanic and you're a really soft car.*

I took a breath, dropped my robe, and leapt onto the table, face-down.

Let Me Start By Saying

She can't see me if I close my eyes, right?

The water turned on, and the room began steaming up. I was chanting to myself *Not Naked Not Naked Not Naked* when I felt the delicate smack of a folded up wet washcloth hit me where the sun usually doesn't shine: in an attempt at modesty, she covered up my butt crack.

Oh yeah, way better now.

The warm sugar scrub she massaged into me with a round wooden brush felt so surprisingly good, I almost relaxed for a few minutes.

Then she moved the Vichy shower into place, and turned on the powerful jets.

Apparently, it is quite therapeutic to pound a woman's spine with rushes of warm water. What is not taken into consideration is that when said woman is not wearing anything on her bottom, the water pressure will make her jellified butt cheeks wiggle violently. No folded-up washcloth can protect a booty from that peculiar sensation.

As I often do in uncomfortable situations, I burst into a fit of giggles. I mean, how is this at all relaxing? Each cheek was doing some Shakira-like solo dance, and the tiny washcloth was sinking into my Great Divide.

The therapist ignored my snorting laughter, moved the jets, and advised me to roll over.

I'm not sure how I didn't see this coming.

It's one thing to let a stranger see your back door. It's another for her to get The Full Monty without at least dinner first.

I Just Want to Pee Alone

Another. Dilemma.

Like an albino rhino covered in lube, I wriggled and twisted to turn myself over, landing with a loud splat in a puddle of vanilla-scented humility.

My biggest side effect of pregnancy was palatial fun bags. Each one was bigger than my head, so I had a choice to make. *Do I use both hands to cover my boobs, or my Downtown Lady Parts? Is my forearm long enough to cover both cans, while the other —*

Problem solved! The therapist tossed a balled-up washcloth at my hoo-ha with the precision of a softball pitcher, and then laid a hand towel across my towering teats. I've had less intimate relationships with PAP-smear technicians.

At this point, I had no choice but to surrender to the music filled with crashing waves (which was totally making me need to pee) while this woman tried her best to scrub me into the ecstasy I had longed for.

When it was all over, and I was back in the safety of my clothes, I met the girls for lunch. While I told them what happened, we all laughed so hard that two years' worth of tension released from my shoulders and I finally felt the relaxation I had hoped to achieve that weekend.

Sure, I had to pay the price of a washcloth colonic and getting smacked in the cookie by a stranger, but I remembered what it was like to feel pampered again. I also realized that it was even more important now to make time for myself as I used to, and maybe I needed to redefine what relaxation means to me these days.

But *man*, was my skin smooth.

Kim Bongiorno is a writer, mom, and wife looking at her suburban life and wondering what the hell just happened. Her blog Let Me Start By Saying *earned her a spot on Circle of Moms Top 25 Funny Moms list in 2011 & 2012, and she has received accolades from the likes of Babble, HuffPostParents, NickMom, and BlogHer.*

Previously published in Fifty Shades of Funny: Hook-Ups, Break-Ups and Crack-Ups, *and the author of the 5-star-rated e-book* Part of My World: Short Stories, *she is currently working on her first Young Adult novel.*

You can find Kim on InThePowderRoom, HuffPostParents, and KimBongiornoWrites.com, when she's not busy making herself laugh with inane updates on Facebook and Twitter.

Kim lives in New Jersey with her handsome husband and two charmingly loud kids.

I Love Disney World.
Wait, No. That Whole Title is a Typo.
By Karen Alpert
Baby Sideburns

Yo, Disney World, WTF happened? I remember when you used to be all fun, and I'd just bounce from ride to ride without a care in the world and everything was free and shit. Like, I could just walk up to a churro stand and say give me a churro and the guy would give me a churro and he'd never ask me for a dime. So when did it all change?

Ohhh yeahhh, when I stopped being the kid and started being the F'ing parent. 'Cause now I'm the one who has to deal with the map, and figure out the whole Fast Pass crap, and pay $9,000 for four ice creams that cost like two cents at Costco, and make sure we use the potty *before* we get in the two-hour line to meet Belle's sister's cousin's housekeeper.

Yup, I found this all out when we were in Florida on vacation and decided to take the kids to Disney World for a day.

Brainless Hubby: I think they'd have a blast. She loves princesses.

Stupid Ass Me: Yeah, Disney is awesome. Why not?

I'll tell you why the fuck not. Because one kid is still in diapers and will purposely poop four times while you're there simply because you have to use changing tables that are literally shat on 24/7/365 days a year, and because the other kid is three-and-a-half and will not live up to her end of the bargain that she has to be happy and grateful and not be a three-and-a-half-year-old little douchebag.

Anyways, after waking up the kiddos two hours early (which should feel awesome because they do that to me every damn day) and driving three hours, we finally get to Magic Kingdom. A friend of mine calls it Meltdown Kingdom and I always thought she was just exaggerating. Not. At. All. Everywhere you look you see hundreds of kids on leashes getting hopped up on sugar and then falling to the ground in tears as their parents try to drag them to the next ride. "I'm gonna count to three young lady and you better start having fun goddamn it."

Our first stop there was the Peter Pan ride. Why? Because the line was only 20 minutes long which is basically as short as a line gets at Disney World. And here is a quick summary of how this ride went:

So first you're flying through this dark room, and then you're flying through this darker room, and then you're flying through a room that's pitch black and then there's a crocodile eating a man, and then your three-and-a-half-year-old is shitting her pants and screaming at the top of her lungs. Well, that was a good way to start the day.

Me: I'm sorry, I'm sorry, honey. Mommy screwed up. I promise this next ride is going to be amazing. And not scary at all.

Daughter: (sobbing) Noooo, I don't want to go on any more rides.

Well, that's awesome. So basically we just paid $300 for a 2 minute Peter Pan ride, but really thousands of dollars considering the months years decades of therapy my kid's gonna need after this.

Next stop, It's a Small World. Yup, there's nothing like watching a bunch of animatronic kiddos from Israel and Iran singing arm-in-arm to cheer you up.

Daughter: Aggggggghhhhhhhhh, nooooooo! There's a crocodile again! Get me the fuck out of Africa!!!!

Yeah, who would have guessed that Africa would have an animatronic crocodile like the one in the Peter Pan ride?

Me: How about the Mad Hatter Tea Cups, sweetie?

Daughter: Yeah! I've always wanted to go on those. (Even though she has no F'ing idea what they are.)

Question: How many gallons of vomit do they clean at the Mad Hatter teacups every year?

Answer: Infinity.

You should have seen her adorable little face light up as it started to spin.

Daughter: I lovvvvvvvve the teacups!!!

OMG, did she LOVE this ride! The first 1/10th of it. And this is what she screamed for the next 9/10ths of the ride.

Daughter: It's too fassssssst! Make it stopppppp!

And when it finally stopped, the people who ran the ride had to peel her out of the teacup where she lay in the fetal position foaming at the mouth.

Of course, there were plenty of things she did love at Disney that day. The Swiss Family Robinson Treehouse (basically just a bunch of stairs, we could have done this for free in an office building), a show with Mickey, Minnie and like 200 princesses (made me throw up in my mouth a little. Correction: *a lot*), the $30 Rapunzel hat we caved and bought for her (anything with fake hair should be illegal), and this giant vending machine in the bathroom that sold tampons and pads. ("Pleeeeeease Mommy can I have one pleeeeease, I'm STARVING!")

And then after we got home from our vacation someone asked her, "What was your favorite thing at Disney World?" And guess what she answered?

Daughter: A Mickey Mouse ice cream bar!

I have one word for you. WTF? I'm not even sure if that's a word. But I'll say it again. WTF?

But yes, all in all, our day at Disney was great. Not at all what I expected (pixie dust, rainbows, unicorns, my daughter hugging characters left and right, my son holding in his poop all day, and not a single tear except for the one that I would shed in complete utter joy). But great nonetheless. A lot like parenthood. Not at all what you expected and full of bumps and hurdles and projectile poops, but still great. Usually. Well, sometimes. Occasionally. Once in a while. Okay, I'll stop there.

Karen Alpert is the ridiculously hairy, self-deprecating writer of the usually funnyish (oh yeah, spell check, then how the F do you spell that?) blog Baby Sideburns. She lives with her two amazing kiddos and a very forgiving husband who's kind enough not to call her "Cousin It" when she undresses for bed every night.

Eat Poop, Laugh.
No, I Did Not Forget a Comma.
By Patti Ford
Insane in the Mom-Brain

Until my son was four, he was at home with me all day, every day. This was a time in our lives when one day felt like ten. Nearly every day spent at home was like that movie *Groundhog Day*, but instead of being awakened by the horrific vocal stylings of Sonny & Cher, I was awakened by a whiney shorty with a poopy diaper. To be honest, I don't know what's worse: crying and crap, or Sonny & Cher. The jury is still out on that. But if you have survived life with a child up until this age, then you know that the days can get a bit monotonous. And by "a bit," I mean that there's so much freaking monotony that sometimes you wanna spork yourself in the eyeball just so you can take a field trip to the hospital to shake things up.

During this time, I was obsessed with having somewhere to go every day. Every. Single. Day. That was the only thing (besides the eyeball sporking) that could change up the routine and make a day go by faster.

One morning, when my son was about three-years-old, I decided to take him to the zoo. It was a spur of the moment decision, brought on by being awakened way the heck before dawn, and already having had a mother-son discussion with him about the importance of actually pooping IN the potty, and not in his pants while standing NEXT TO the potty. Not to mention, I'd already lost at least 11,274 more brain cells from listening to Caillou whine like the little, bald, bitch that he is.

I seriously had to get out of that house. And since, for some stupid reason, it's illegal for a mother to leave her child home alone, even if he's clearly shown that he's a helluva lot smarter than her, I had to plan a trip for two. Sometimes it's just best not to be home alone with a child who was seemingly sent to this earth for the sole purpose of finding your breaking point. Every now and again you honestly need the prying eyes of the public so that you don't duct tape your spawn to the ceiling fan, in the hopes that it "gently" lulls them to sleep.

Normally I would plan out these little sanity-saving excursions ahead of time by sending an email to my friends on Sunday so that we could organize our outings for the week. To observers, I'm sure we looked like an amazingly awesome and organized group of Super Moms, taking our kids here and there and giving them social time, fresh air, and fun experiences. In reality, those things were just a lucky by-product of something that we were actually doing in order to keep us from finally snapping and pawning our wedding rings for a one-way plane ticket to Fiji.

This time I didn't plan things out and I didn't have time to invite friends. We just got the hell out of Dodge.

On the 30 minute drive to the zoo, we listened to "Tappy Tappin' With Elmo," approximately 10.3 times, which made the journey extra harrowing and long. Seriously, Frodo's trip to Middle Earth seemed like a breeze in comparison. Giant spiders and big, murdery, bird thingies? Bitch, puhleeze. I see your big-ass walking trees and raise you a squeaky, red, puppet voice that never freaking stops. By the time we arrived at the zoo and I finally found a parking spot, my brain was pretty much liquefied. When I got out of the car and opened the back door to grab The Boy, I discovered that he wasn't wearing any pants. Or shoes. You might think that since he was a three-year-old, and three-year-olds are total a-holes, he just stripped himself of the claustrophobic confines of his clothes while he was in the back seat jammin' out to Elmo. That wouldn't be the first or 100th time that he had decided to be free of fabric on a whim. That little dude liked nothing more than letting his stuff get some air. But after looking around the backseat for a while, I realized that for once he *wasn't* practicing for his future as a stripper, and that in my crazy "Momma's about to lose her mind, up in here, up in here" dash to get out of the house, I had completely forgotten about an important little thing called clothes.

This is one of the many odd and unexpected little situations where you kinda find out who you are as a mother. Will you collapse onto the parking lot in the fetal position and cry for the days when you had perky boobs, bladder control, and alone time? Or will you laugh because you see the funny in being a spaced out, overwhelmed, mess? It's got to be a test masterminded by the aliens who stole you out of your bed that night four years ago, and impregnated you with this annoying little creature that likes to eat chalk, and write on his chalkboard with ketchup. You know they're just floating around up there in their UFO, waiting on pins and needles to see how their human subject is going to react in the latest edition of an ongoing experiment called, "How much can one human mother take until she totally and completely loses her shit?"

This was *at least* the 80-bazillionth time that I had been given this test in keeping my sanity. My passes and fails had probably been a pretty equal split so far.

The first time I nearly lost my mind was long before The Boy had vacated my belly. He was still mooching off of me, and doing everything within his power to drive me insane. Not only was I so sick that I had to crawl everywhere because I couldn't even stand up without getting vomitty, but I was fat, my boobs hurt, my gums were bleeding, and my brain (like my only barf-free mode of transportation) had regressed to that of a two-year-old. I was also constipated, had hemorrhoids the size of a fist, and my uterus was being kicked like it was the set of a mother-flippin' Jean Claude Van Damme movie. The Boy was HUGE and he insisted on trying to flip himself over even though he was way beyond the acceptable, or physically possible, size for that crap.

The second time I nearly lost my mind was when I was finally getting to push the giant parasite out, and reclaim my body once and for all. The only thing that I can possibly say about that experience within the allotted space that I have here is this: *Holymotherfuckingbullshitfromhelltimesamillion.* That DID NOT go as planned. Oh, and I will give you just seven more words: My hospital room had to be repainted.

You can use your imaginations on that one.

The third time I nearly lost it was when The Hub and I brought The Boy home from the hospital. We honestly marveled at how passive he was, even high-fiving each other for having such a perfect peach of a baby. We were totally rockin' this procreation situation, and we felt like the luckiest bastards on the planet. That is, until a few days later, when his *real* personality came out and we considered a middle of the night, top-secret move to Lithuania, or somewhere just as equally nowhere.

There had been many more times like these, when I thought that I was going to spontaneously combust from the exhaustion and aggravation. Times when I would have possibly even welcomed combustion, because not only would that be an excitingly kick-ass way to exit the planet, but also a way to end the sleepless stressfest, that is motherhood.

But there is a key to handling everything from accidentally eating a blob of poop off your hand that in the sleepless, zombie-like state of new mommyhood, you thought was chocolate, all the way to experiencing the wrath of the check out lady at Target who looks like she seriously wants to kick your ass because your child just told her that he has a sister (which he doesn't) that you keep locked in the attic (which you don't).

That key is humor.

I have absolutely zero concept of how anyone without a sense of humor can actually survive the task of raising a child, or for that matter, how a child can survive *being* raised by a bummer of a parent. When you're a mom, crazy shit happens every single day. Your child will do things that you would probably beat the crap out of a grown-up person for doing. They will destroy everything of value. They will shit on your floors. They will draw on your walls. They will spill drinks on every upholstered item in your home. They will vomit on your clothes. They will swallow your earring, and shove a blueberry in their ear. They will refuse to wear anything other than some stupid Peter Pan costume and their froggy rain boots to the store with you. When you *get* to the store, they will go balls to the wall, Shirley MacLaine/*Terms of Endearment* CRAZY in the cookie aisle if you won't let them have a freakin' bag of Oreos. They will also drop trou in the crowded play land of a local restaurant, and shake their moneymaker like there's no tomorrow.

But they will also love you no matter what. Even if you yell at them. Even if you spank them. Even if you say "no" to the cookies. They will love you even if you cry, look like hell, and accidentally eat some of their poop.

So you *have to* laugh. You have to laugh at these little creatures and all the shit they pull and the tantrums they throw. You *have to* think of it as Personality Training 101. Not for them, but for you. And you have to realize that even if they sometimes drive you so insane that you can't even remember to put pants and shoes on them before you take them out in public, *that* shit is priceless. Plus, there's a Target three blocks away, and a funny story to tell when they grow up. And when you tell it to them then, they will laugh their butt off, because they will have a good sense of humor. Just like their poop-eating mom.

Patti is a wife, mom, blogger, cook, cat box scooper, and dirty underwear picker upper. In her spare time, she performs musicals for her cat, daydreams about owning her own unicorn ranch, prepares for the Zombie Apocalypse, and practices her Karate Kid Crane Kick. Someday she hopes to own a miniature donkey that she can dress up like a dandy English gentleman. She will call this donkey Duke Dudesbury Donkelson III. You can read her blog at www.insanemombrain.com.

Kids and Cleaning: Just Kill Me Now
By Teri Biebel
Snarkfest

I don't understand the way kids think, especially when it comes to cleaning. You know what I'm talking about. You tell your teenager to clean her room. An hour later, you check on her and not *one* thing has changed about the condition of her room.

However, she *was* finally able to find her yearbook from 5th grade and has spent the better part of the last hour pouring over it and laughing at how dorky everyone looked. And for crying out loud, how many times does a teenager have to be taught that in addition to clothes being washed and dried, they also need to be *folded* and *put away*?!?!

Hey daughter, you know that big thing that you precariously pile all your shit on? You know the one I mean. There's a mirror attached to it that you use every day to look at yourself (once you move all the shit piled on top to one side). The long rectangular one with about eight tons of girl shit piled on top of it. Yeah, that thing we bought you that had a matching desk and headboard. That's for clean clothes. No, the floor wasn't meant for clean clothes Or dirty clothes, Einstein. No, putting them on your bed, then "accidentally" knocking them onto the floor *does not* count as "putting your damn clothes away." And another thing. It's called a goddamn clothes hamper. Don't be afraid to use it!!

In one particularly memorable moment, my oldest, 15, decided that all of her tee shirts should be hung on hangers in her closet. Tee shirts. Tee-*flipping*-shirts, taking up every clothes hanger in my neighborhood, hanging in her closet. Sweaters? On the floor. Pants? Floor. Socks? Undies? Bras? Floor, floor, floor. But damn, those tee shirts look good hanging in the closet!

Not impressed yet? How about the fact that she had them all lined up according to color??? What the bloody snot is that???? It was like a My Little Pony threw up in her closet with all the shades of red, orange, yellow, green . . . You get the idea. All colors grouped together, going from lightest to darkest. Good Lord. Why for the love of God can she spend time doing that, but not putting her shit in her dresser?? Does she not realize how much extra time that takes up? Time better spent, oh, I dunno, looking for your fucking floor???

Let's move onto the kitchen, shall we? Because I'm going to have an aneurysm if I concentrate much longer on her bedroom. I'm going to start with the dishes. My oldest child has no issue letting the dogs kiss her on the face, she'll eat food off the floor (*five second rule!!*) and has no issue with eating a cheese stick that has been sitting in her lunch bag for two straight weeks.

However, ask that same child to load the dishwasher and you'd think I'd just asked her to perform a colonoscopy on the cat using a straw and a flashlight. The kid has to put on Playtex rubber gloves because God forbid she should touch a fork that's been in someone else's mouth. Pay no mind to the fact that it's her mother's fork. The same fork that she just used to take a bite of her mother's food. In the mouth is okay, but touching it with bare hands is a fate worse than death. She is grossed out to the point of nausea. And for crying out loud, why does it take an hour to load six dinner forks, five dirty bowls, four spoons, three juice glasses, two knives, and a coffee mug in a pear tree? Oh, maybe because she is like a cat with a laser pointer. One fork in, then *oooooh shiny!!* Back to the dishwasher, rinse a plate, load it into the dishwasher, and then ooooooh is that One Direction on the computer? It is pointless to have the oldest load the dishwasher if the youngest is on the computer, because nothing productive will ever get accomplished. It will continue to be a steady stream of one fork in, one

"Hey come here and look at this!" It makes me scream. And it doesn't matter how many times I ask: in her mind, that plate is obviously going to walk itself over to the sink, rinse itself off and load itself into the dishwasher if it's left on the table long enough. Just ask my oldest. She "forgets" every night to take her plate from the table, rinse it and put it in the dishwasher. Every. Single. Night. And the next morning, it's magically off the table and in the dishwasher. It's like magic! I truly fear for her future husband. That kid had better marry money so she can hire a maid, because I'm certainly not moving in with her. I spend my nights trying to imagine how many college roommates she's going to piss off with her slovenly habits. I can hear them now. "Ew, you're a pig. Didn't your mom ever teach you how to clean??" and I'm positive she's going to say "Nope, she never did." I could just scream.

Now that I've gotten my blood pressure up above stroke level, let's move onto the family room, or as I like to call it, "Shit Central." Got shit? You've come to the right place. If I were to invite you over and say "Wanna sit on my love seat?" I'd have to follow it up with "Sorry, you're gonna have to move that hoodie, the basketball, the gym bag, the book bag, and the three week's worth of newspapers that my husband has left sitting there." Crap, let's go sit at the kitchen table. No, wait, dirty dishes still abound there. OK back to Shit Central, we can always move the dogs off the couch and sit there. I'd tell you to put your wine glass down on one of the end tables, but those are covered with paper from last month's science fair project, tape, scissors, glue sticks and, would you look at that? More newspapers. Seriously, husband? What the hell is the problem? When you're finished in the bathroom, you get rid of that shit, right? So when you're finished reading the paper, can't you follow that same line of thinking? It's not rocket science. It's called a paper bag. We recycle. This isn't new. Put the papers in the bag. I'll ask the oldest to put the bag of recycled newspapers in the garage, and oh, wait, while she's doing that, perhaps she could remove the basketball from my loveseat and put *that* out in the garage where we *normally* keep all sporting equipment. Oh sorry, not enough hands. Oh, sorry, I was just out in the garage, I don't feel like making a second trip with the basketball. I suppose it would be considered child abuse to throw said basketball at said teenager's head, right?

Fuck it, can we just go to your house? I'm sure it's cleaner there. And even if it's not, I don't care, because at least *my* kids don't live there!

I'm Teri Biebel, and I was born in Philly, and raised in Jersey. I'm 45 years old, and after working 24 years in the casino industry, I wanted nothing more to do with slot machines, table games, and stealing people blind, so I left for the private sector. I'm married to Don and have two amazing (and trying) teens, 15 and 13. I spend most of my time living like a circus clown, juggling schedules and chauffeuring large groups of people in a five-passenger car. I am sarcastic, I am snarky and my oldest has coined the term 'Snarkastic' to describe me. People tell me that I'm funny and as long they don't follow that up with the word "looking" I'm totally okay with it. You can read more of my writing on my blog, <u>Snarkfest</u>.

Love, Tears, and a Few Scattered Ashes
By Meredith Spidel
The Mom of the Year

Nine months ago, my mother died. This was the saddest, most painful time of my life, but somehow unexpected laughter managed to eke its way into the days and moments following her death. It was such a sweet and surprising blessing to find shards of levity within the despair. As it turns out, a good snort can go very far in navigating through loads of weirdness and hurt.

The awkward funny began literally the second she passed from this world. You see, we thought she was dead, but we weren't quite sure. My husband had taken the kids home because it had been a long day, and my dad, sister, brother-in-law and I were settled in on the living room couch pretending to read and leaf through magazines. *What is, exactly, the protocol for sitting bedside with your dying mom who has been unresponsive for hours?* All of the sudden, sister elbow-punched my brother-in-law. We all looked at my mother, who appeared not to be breathing any more. Her breathing had become so shallow by this point, we couldn't tell if she actually stopped.

What now? Someone had the idea of putting a pocket mirror under her nose to see if the glass fogged like I used to do in those paranoid days of early motherhood with my babies, but that didn't work well. I called hospice, "Hi, I'm here with MaryAnn and we think she may have died." They said they would send someone out in 45 minutes. *Super. Thanks, we'll just sit here for the next three-quarters of an hour with our possibly dead mother.*

It then dawned on us that we could check for her pulse (yes, this should have occurred to us first, but apparently capacity to think clearly flees in close proximity of a dead loved one), except no one wanted to do it. Touching a maybe-dead body can be a very freaky thing. My sister finally made my brother-in-law do it, promising to someday return the favor if ever necessary with his parents. Thus, a new family standard was established: in event of questionable death, in-laws will be responsible for all hands-on body-checks.

After determining that she was, in fact, dead, my father, a very practical man, took the opportunity to finish up some laundry he had been working on. *Of course, Dad. Might as well make good use of the time.* Somehow this didn't seem that completely weird until he brought the laundry back in the living room and started folding it onto piles on every available surface—including my mother's body. *Cue open-mouth gaping.* It is important to note that our faith does not value the physical body after a person has passed, but still, this seemed a bit extreme. Nothing screams inappropriate like, "Mind grabbing that pile of towels off of Mom's legs? The fresh tee-shirts are over by her arms."

A series of coroners, hospice, and undertakers later, my sister and I then decided to spend the night. I asked my father if he had any extra pillows. He looked around and eying the ones on my mother's hospital bed, handed them to me. Aghast, I shrieked, "My mother just died on those!" Somehow, pillows managed to be conjured up from some more neutral location in the house.

Fast forward through a couple awkward, but nice-to-be-with-family days and a loooong group trip to Kohls to buy my dad, a man who does NOT shop, his first new suit in years and proper funeral dresses for my sister and me (*What precisely should one wear to her mother's funeral?*), and we found ourselves at the day of the service.

My mother had been cremated, and the plan was to bury her ashes in the ground of a memorial garden at the church. Having never buried ashes before, we weren't sure what exactly to expect. We assumed we would just be placing the entire urn in a hole. We were wrong. Very wrong. After some lovely words of commemoration, the pastor indicated we were to actually transfer the ashes from the urn into the hole in the ground. There was no scoop in sight. This urn was massive. Huge. *Dawning realization set in quickly: we were supposed to use our hands to grab the remains of my mother and throw them in the ground?! What surprising great news. So glad I wore heels for the occasion.*

My brave father went first and threw in a handful. I went next. Then it was my sister's turn. She threw in a handful and stopped. We had a problem. We had about 15 tons of our dead mother's ashes and we were fresh out of immediate family members. She started to grab several quick handfuls, but it became apparent that we would be there for months on end at this rate. So the dear girl squatted, grabbed up that bad boy of an urn, upturned it and started to shake it out. Being the very helpful older sister that I am, I jumped right in and said, "Here, let me hold your purse." She shot me hateful daggers and continued shaking our mother into the ground. Hey, sometimes it just sucks to be the youngest. At least I had the purses covered.

That March day was one of the windiest ever. As it turns out, white ashes and black dresses don't work so well. After my mother was successfully interred in the ground, we made quick work towards the bathroom. I got there first and was busy paper-toweling the ash off me when my sister entered. I asked, "Coming in to wash mom off you?" We keeled over in hysterical laughter and couldn't stop. There is something tragically perfect about trying to sponge your dead mother's ashes off your dress with crappy church bathroom paper towels right before going into her memorial service. I can't imagine what people must have thought about MaryAnn's crazy daughters laughing like lunatics before the funeral. The proudest moment of the day.

Post-service, we gathered for a "receiving line" and got to chat with some very sweet people who genuinely loved my mother and wanted to support us. As I've learned, though, not everyone is able to express their concern eloquently. There was the man who told us he "earned" at least a couple of sandwiches by sitting through the service. *Classy. Let me know your going rate for funeral attendance. I have some upcoming services I'd love to book you for, and I'll need to get the proper number of sandwiches ready.*

There was the friend who told me my earrings looked "so slutty." *Um, thanks. And since I'm not vulnerable or anything right now, I will handle this comment extremely well without getting upset or paranoid about it all.*

And then there was the family who congratulated me on my pregnancy and asked when the baby was due. My daughter was seven months old at this point and another pregnancy was very, very far off our radar. *Fantastic. I appreciate the head's up that my body is a disaster. I'll just pop over to the gym after the service with all the extra energy I have right now and get to work on that.*

When everyone finally finished pouring out these sweet sentiments and it was time to go home, my sister's friend (who I love dearly) was walking out to the car with us. She then realized she had locked her keys in the car. *Of course.* Of course, we would then find ourselves sitting around my parents' kitchen table, making cheerful post-service small talk waiting for AAA to call her back within hours after putting my mother in the ground. Because really, what would any mom's funeral be without a need for AAA?

I would trade almost anything to still have my mother here on this earth, but I am grateful for all of these ridiculous laughs that helped carry my family through this time. I like to think of these nearly-peeing-my-pants moments as one of my mom's final gifts to me, and am cherishing all of these memories. It was a horrible time, but it was also a horribly funny time. Here's to you, Mom.

Meredith blogs at The Mom of the Year*, dedicatedly earning her title one epic parenting fail at a time. When her kids aren't busy pummeling each other with Legos or requiring their 16th sippy cup refill of the day, she tries to offer quick, relatable laughs for fellow parents of the world and all their empathizers. She remains entirely terrified by crafts, promises to never share any useful household tips, and is fully committed to a less serious look at the world of parenting.*

Why I Belong in Coach
By Julianna W. Miner
Rants from Mommyland

I'm sitting on a plane in first class for the very first time. All the people walking past me have no idea that I don't fly first class all the time. Continue your sad shuffling to the back of the plane, people. I'll be here sipping champagne and taking my extra legroom for granted. I settle in, feeling superior and glamorous (and like I didn't just spend most of the afternoon trying to get cat puke out of my dining room rug). I look across the aisle. There is a large man; attractive in a growly, possibly dangerous kind of way. He looks exactly like that famous actor . . . What's his name? Oh my sweet baby condor. It really is him. Holy Shit.

How long has he been sitting there? Did it look like I was picking my nose a minute ago when I scratched it? No. I scratched it. Really. Did he just think he saw me pick my nose? Why am I going to vomit all of a sudden? He glances at me and sees that I am gaping at him, mouth open, eyes big, all traces of dignity and tact long gone. I close my mouth very quickly and unfortunately it makes a noise when it shuts. Good that my mouth is now closed in case I throw up.

He smiles curtly at me, as if to say: please stop looking at me, I acknowledged you, now look away or I will have you escorted back to coach with the rest of the carnie folk. I try to give him a brief smile back, indicating that I totally get it. But somehow, I don't think it looked very nice, because he suddenly seems concerned and alarmed, as if I am about to have a seizure. He quickly looks away.

Shit. Why was I not aware of his presence? I sat there for maybe five minutes and wasn't sucking in my stomach. I saw that movie with him and his abs. I should have had some intuitive female response to his presence, even if I couldn't see him. I mean there would obviously have been a major testosterone spike as soon as he showed up, right? Have I been married that long? Has motherhood deadened my response to such powerful pheromones? Is that possible?

God damn it. What the hell is wrong with me?! Get it together, for Christ's Sake. And stop taking the name of the Lord in vain, you asshole.

Wait a minute. Did I just say that last part out loud? Oh Lord. Oh no. I think I did.

Well, that is just *perfect*. Before I even have the opportunity to figure out how to deal with sitting four feet from this specimen, I have to make an ass of myself. Of course, if I had tricked him into thinking I was normal, clever or charming, when I eventually outed myself, it would surely have been much worse. Right? I mean I could have chatted with him for a while. Asked him where he was going or casually mentioned that I was a writer (leaving off the part about it only being for the internet). And he might have sort of liked me for a few minutes.

And then I would invariably say some jackass thing, (or perhaps have thrown up on him?) and then the look of horror and revulsion on his face, caused by me, in front of all the deserving first class passengers . . . That would have been much harder to deal with. Now he just thinks I'm odd but not a complete psycho. That's something.

Wait a minute; I know what I'll do. I will start reading stuff for work. I will be interpreted as being a very serious and intelligent professional woman. I'll highlight stuff and write comments in the margins and make very quiet tsk tsk noises. Let's see how that goes . . .

It's very hard to concentrate on this stupid stuff. Was I ever able to read? Because I can't now. I can only stare at the same page and sneak the occasional look at him. Did he just glance at me? Why am I sweating now? I'm actually stress sweating. Wait. Did I put on deodorant this morning? *Of course not.* Great, I smell like I'm from Belgium.

I may need to re-think this strategy. The quieter I am, the easier it is for him to ignore my presence. I mean, *why on earth* would he want to do that? Here I am, attractive (in a plump, slightly mommish kind of way). I am obviously happily married and settled with kids (having the appropriate rings and enormous handbag to prove it). I am clearly mentally deranged (as evidenced by talking aloud to myself before take off). *Am I not perfect for him?*

More and more he seems to be focusing on the rather attractive airline attendant that keeps bringing him drinks and flirting with him. Size two with big boobs. And a southern accent. Oh please. Is that for real? She is not my favorite.

She keeps talking. I don't like her at all. Not because she is flirting (successfully) with him. But because she is an affront to all women, and all blondes, and all southern belles, and all flight attendants. She may be hot, but really what about *feminism*?! Wait. The part about me judging her because of how she looks and the fact she's acting sort of crazy around this man? I'm being assholish. I remember being in my twenties and single. Sort of. It was a long time ago.

I Just Want to Pee Alone

I wonder if anyone else is noticing what's going on between these two. Oh yeah! All the men in first class are smiling at her and looking smug. All the women are avoiding eye contact. What is really going on here? I'm suddenly afraid we're watching a little show where this young woman arranges an impersonal sexual encounter with this famous actor and we all watch it go down like we're part of some voyeuristic Mile High Club.

No, thank you. I wish I were back in coach with my people. My people don't do this sort of thing. Who was I kidding? I am not some first class, fancy-pants person. *I fly coach.* This is just nauseating.

Well if he goes for that sort of thing then I am not watching his abs ever again. Probably. That'll show him. For all he knows I could be a well connected, moneyed type of person who flies first class all the time. And if I were one of those people, then I would be *eccentric* and not *psychotic*. Then his disgraceful conduct and the fact that he is stupidly and meanly ignoring me would be wrong.

Doesn't he know that he is supposed to start up a conversation with me? And from our instant and natural rapport flows an exchange so meaningful as to cause him to fall deeply in love with me? That of course would lead to him propositioning me with sex and possibly marriage, which of course I would delicately deny him, while also searing my lovely, brilliant, and demure image into his memory. So that at age 85 when writing his memoirs I am mentioned several times as the only woman who could have ever made him happy? What is wrong with him? Here I am *right across the aisle* and still, nothing, no playful banter, no longing glances, nothing.

Sigh . . . This whole thing makes me sick. I am going to the bathroom where I at least don't have to watch this anymore.

As I wash my hands and prepare to re-apply lipstick, I - *Oh dear.* How long ago was lunch? Good God. I have been walking around for 3 hours and 45 minutes with a stain on my shirt directly over my nipple. It's disgusting. It looks exactly like my left boob is leaking. And the stain is crusty. And I don't even know what's worse – that the stain is there and he hasn't noticed because he hasn't looked at my tits even once or that in one glance, he was able to ascertain that I am in fact a giant boobstain. I feel like screaming *"Yes! I am a boobstain! You should know that about me! I think it's low fat ranch! But we should still be friends!"*

I return to my seat with my face a shade of red usually reserved for hot rods and tomatoes. This is the worst flight I have ever been on. This is stomach churning torture. And to make matters worse, the Daughter of the Confederacy stewardess is STILL THERE. Oh I give up.

Wait a minute. He just said thank you and then sort of turned his back on her. Now he appears to be reading something. Can it be? That he is actually a sweet man? Who flirted with her only because he didn't want to be rude? Now he wants to read and be left alone?

Oh look . . . He's falling asleep. How cute is he? Oh no. I shouldn't watch him sleep. This poor man, with all these people watching while he's trying to rest. Does he know that everyone is looking at him while he sleeps? This is sort of gross. I am watching him sleep and for some reason it makes me feel dirty. And not in a good way. I resolve not to look at him again.

I am not looking at him.

Hours pass and I am not looking at him.

I Just Want to Pee Alone

Actually only about six minutes have passed.

This is kind of hard. I sigh and look at my watch again. We're landing soon. My window of opportunity is almost over. No one is going to believe that he was sitting right next to me. I can't take a picture of him with my phone without everyone seeing me and besides, doing it while he's sleeping just feels yucky.

We're descending. He's still crashed out. I start to panic. In a minute he will walk off this plane and the next time I see him he'll be 10 feet tall, projected onto a wall in suburban Washington, DC.

We're landing and he's awake. Damn it. I missed my chance. Why couldn't have I said something clever? Why did I have to get shy, subverting my normally obstreperous personality? I could have at least stammered out something. Even something knuckle-headed like "Uh . . . Omigod! You're that guy! You were so good in that movie with your abs!" (To which he would have assuredly responded with "Bugger off!" or some other tough and foreign sounding obscenity.) That at least would be something I could brag about to my friends ("Did you hear about the time that actor told me to 'bugger off' in first class?? Hee hee hee!") But no, I didn't even get that.

We're walking off the plane, through the tube toward the terminal, crowded together like cattle. I almost feel like crying. I wish I could have just said something to him. Anything at all. You know what? I will! I am going to turn around and say something to him before some Playboy Bunny Supermodel girlfriend meets him, beautiful, and open-armed at the gate.

A couple of business men rudely push their way past me. Well, I don't care how crowded and unpleasant this is, I am going to say something to him before I lose my chance forever. I turn around to make my move as I feel a hand (and for certain it's a *hand*, not a suitcase or carry-on) brush against my rear end and give it a little nudge. I turn around, and he smiles at me sheepishly and says, "Pardon me. Terribly sorry."

He touched my ass.

Damn . . . I knew he loved me.

Julianna W. Miner writes the successful humor blog <u>Rants from Mommyland</u>. *She has also written for* Babble, The Huffington Post, The Washington Times *Communities, and Nickelodeon ParentsConnect.*

She has three kids, two jobs, a long-suffering husband, a dog who should be ashamed of himself and a geriatric, ill-tempered cat. In addition to blogging, she teaches at a college she couldn't have gotten into because she made bad choices in high school. She writes about how hard it is to raise kind-hearted, successful, and happy kids while constantly having to wipe things and pick up dirty socks.

In the Name of the Father, the Son, and the Holy Penis
By Bethany Thies
Bad Parenting Moments

Shortly after the birth of our fourth child, my husband and I sat down to discuss our birth control options. I was a few days shy of my six week postpartum check-up. At this appointment, after the careful poking and prodding of your barely healed nether regions, the inevitable topic of birth control comes up.

Physician: "So, what are you currently using for birth control?"

Me: "Besides wishes and dreams? Oh, well...I find the best method of birth control is complete abstinence. Wouldn't you agree, Doctor?"

Physician: *[uncomfortable chuckle]* "Well, I'm not sure your spouse would agree. Are you interested in trying *[insert name of birth control pill pharmaceutical representative just pushed over bagels]*?"

Me: "Well, I was thinking that you may just consider officially condemning my vagina as a war zone. I'd hate for anyone to be injured with all of the vaginal shrapnel."

Physician: *[mouthing vaginal shrapnel]* "So, are you interested in an IUD?"

Me: "I find it best never to owe people money. Especially family. IOU's can be so tricky."

Physician: "I have a feeling you may not be ready to discuss any vaginal procedures."

Me: "Hasn't my vagina done enough for my family?"

To be blunt, that is my feeling about birth control. After four vaginal births, my vagina would like to retire. With a watch, "Thank you for your cervix and service!" plaque, and, an impromptu conference room fete thrown by my vaginal associates.

This is why I pushed and my husband, eventually and begrudgingly, agreed to a vasectomy.

Several grueling months of impassioned reminders (see synonym: *nagging*) later, the consultation with the urologist was on the books. Never had my reproductive retirement soiree seemed so near. Then, I made the mistake of inviting a Catholic Priest to dinner.

What happens when you invite a Catholic Priest to dinner? They eat your food, drink your wine and tell your husband he can not have a vasectomy.

It is times like these that I thank God I am not Catholic. I was pouring a glass of red when this commandment was spoken. "Catholics don't do *that*. You can use the rhythm method." As he said, "rhythm method," I pointed to baby number four. *Any other pearls of wisdom, Father?* The conversation soured as I glared at my husband over loudly chewed bites of steak. Looking at my knife, I pondered if Googling DIY vasectomy instruction would initiate any red flags or calls to the local authorities.

My husband, not necessarily a believer in the actual tenet of no vasectomy, yet, thankful for an argument against it tried to proceed cautiously.

Husband: "Did you hear what Father said about [*ahem*] the surgery?"

Me: "I did."

I Just Want to Pee Alone

Husband: "And?"

Me: "Are priests still unable to get married? Unless you plan on marrying him, I think you should consider keeping your appointment."

Husband: "Honey, please put down the steak knife."

Although my husband is a committed Catholic, he is more committed to limits we've set as a family. He is committed to me. Besides, while God may be all around us and inside our hearts, I remain unconvinced that God has taken up residence in our pants making sure all the Holy balls are left un-snipped. I think She probably has bigger fish to fry.

Vagina 1, Catholicism 0.

Bethany Thies is a mother of four, writer and rehabilitated gypsy who now calls Vermont home. She can change a diaper in 22 seconds and is the proud author of the chronic sarcasm and tom-foolery blog, <u>Bad Parenting Moments</u>.

A Cougar is Born
By Andrea
Underachiever's Guide to Being a Domestic Goddess

Well, believe it or not, I am about to turn 40. They say 40 is the new 30. Or is it 50 is the new 40? What about "life begins at 40?" No, I think the last time I checked, life begins at birth. I don't even know what they say these days or what any of that means. All I know is "they" have been a pain in my ass for years. "They" are the same people that said red wine is good for you, and then said red wine is bad for you, coffee is a must for good health, oh wait, coffee is terrible on your system, do take aspirin, no, don't take aspirin - and endless other contradictions. Anyhow - I'm turning 40, and damn it I'm going to embrace it – no matter what "they" say!

So what goes along with turning 40? An excuse to celebrate. Why do we feel like we even *need* an excuse? I don't know - mommy guilt, maybe? It's silly, really. I think many of us with young kids hide behind that excuse because quite honestly, it takes a lot less effort to just hang out on the fluffy couch in our loungewear and fuzzy socks, hair in a ponytail, and yesterday's makeup smudged under our eyes than getting ready to go out. It's true. *Everything* takes effort now. So while many of us are complaining that we have no social life because we have no babysitter, or feel like these childhood days are fleeting and we should be home with our kids, we're actually thinking it's much easier to not have to apply ourselves and just stay home!

OK now that I've said that, I realize that because I am fortunate enough to have some really adoring, wonderful, fun-loving friends, I simply cannot - *not* go out for my 40th. This is not going to be a one-stop party and done - it's going to be dinners here and there with this group of friends, drinks with another group of friends. Yes, I plan to milk it for everything it's worth. You only turn 40 once! I'm sure a night out with my husband is on the agenda as well. Well, it had *better* be! Overall, I'm thinking at least a half a dozen 40th Birthday celebrations are in order. Seems only proper to mark the milestone wouldn't you say? I mean what other big milestone is there after you turn 40? Retirement? Selling your home and moving to an assisted living community in Florida? Fiftieth wedding anniversary/acceptance into Sainthood? Nope. This is it - the one big opportunity to go big while we've still "got it." I want parties and lots of them. Let's do it.

What does this mean for me? This means I have some serious work to do to make myself look fabulous. You know, I have to give everyone the impression that I've got 40 under control and I'm not panic stricken by any means. I have to exude that "Forty and Fabulous" feeling when I'm with other ladies my age and younger. Little do they know that behind the scenes, it's more like "Forty and Frumpy." Gone are the days of no make up and still looking presentable. I can no longer get away with a quick jaunt out without a bra for fear of tripping over a boob that has been overused and overstretched by three children. I can't just "throw on" something adorable and get away with it. Nope. These days, it takes *work* - and lots of it to not only look feminine again, but fantastic.

Remember going out in our roaring 20s? We took our time because we didn't have someone yelling that their butt needed wiped in another room, or that they needed a snack, or that the batteries on their Leap Pad are dead and there was an impending meltdown on the horizon. No. We put on some fun music, poured a glass of wine, took a long hot shower and enjoyed getting ready. If we ran late, it was usually because we changed our outfit five times because we either had way too many cute things to choose from, or we were suffering from PMS and didn't like the way something looked, or we weren't sure what the appropriate attire was for the party we were attending. Now, at 40, we have two outfits that look like they are in style, and one that fits if we're lucky - so we're not worried about running late because of too many chic choices. No - if we run late now, it's because we caught a glance of ourselves in the rearview mirror while starting the car and saw a rogue chin hair that we didn't manage to see while in the bathroom.

Why is it the car mirror shows every single lip and chin hair long and dark as can be yet there was no sign of it ten minutes ago in the bathroom? Now, if we don't have tweezers in the car, we've got to run back inside and take care of business . . . which will probably mean three more curveballs to set us back another 10 minutes.

But let's back up a bit. Ok, so we have plans to go out. Right? Now, we have to figure out all of the things we have to do to look like we've got 40 by the family jewels. What does this entail? This involves starting with the shower. Not just any shower. The kind of shower where an emergency, code red level of maintenance must occur. Shampooing, conditioning with serious hair repair, exfoliating, shaving, scrubbing, buffing, and rinsing is happening and you are just getting warmed up. Now we need body butter, moisturizer, and smoothing lotions with a touch of spray to smell pretty. On to the face work. Whatever you do - don't look in one of those magnifying mirrors from Brookstone. You'll never make it out of the house. It's like a horror show when you see all of the renegade hairs on your face, clogged pores filled with old make up from when you last went out two years ago, and dark circles under your eyes that you mistake for makeup and try to remove with make up remover pads only to find they are not actually removable. So we've tweezed, snipped, and shaped eyebrows, lips, face, and neck – we can't forget the neck now that we're 40! We've patted on tinted moisturizer, under eye cream, primer, and bronzer. Hopefully, we've now covered up all signs that we haven't slept in eight years and that we never took care of our skin in our 20s and 30s. Hopefully our skin tone looks like we are well-hydrated even though we've starved ourselves for days to get rid of the sodium bloated look on our faces from staying up late watching bad TV and eating too many salty snacks. Mmmmm . . . salty snacks. Where was I? Yes. Makeup. Now apply lip plumper, primer, liner, and gloss to cover up our dry cracked lips and draw attention away from our double chins. Apply, or try to remember how to apply a nice base of eye shadow in a neutral color so it doesn't appear we are trying *too* hard, yet still get the pop we are all hoping for in our eye makeup. Apply a nice coat of liner that doesn't resemble Tammy Faye Baker and enough coats of mascara to show we do care enough to apply some, but don't want to look like a tarantula.

On to hair. You know - that stuff that keeps your head warm that you tie up in a bun most days to stay out of your way . . . and the stuff that you cover up with a hat when you have to go to the pick up line at your kids' school to appear stylish while covering up the fact that you haven't showered in days. Yes, we'll need to work at the hair a little bit more than usual. Apply an anti-frizz product, volumizer, and smoother all while flipping upside down to ensure body and lift - take a mascara wand to cover the stray grays if you didn't have time to color, and work those jiggly arms while blowing it dry. Throw a few curls via curling iron, hot rollers, flat iron - whatever suits you. Tease up the back a little - but be careful not to over do it because you do not want the Amy Winehouse/Adele/ Flo the Progressive Girl type of pouf-bouffant look. Not attractive at any age.

OK, so shower, lube oil and filter - check. Makeup application - check. Hair styled and shiny - check. Time to put on that one outfit we have that works - or that new outfit that we went and bought just for tonight. Before we put those lovely clothes on though, we have to get the holy trinity of intimate wear . . . you know - Spanx, Booblifters or Boobsmashers (Minimizer Bra or Miracle Bra - depends on how things are shaping up in that department), and control top panty hose. If we were lucky, and planned right, some of these might be combined together like a Spanx-topped pair of stockings or some other type of similar torture device. Anyhow - suck it up, squeeze in, suck it in, smash it, lift it, separate it - do what we have to do. No one said beauty is painless.

Got all of our contraptions fastened? Good. Put on the outfit. Ahh, look how nice everything looks! Now, add some sparkly, dangly earrings that draw attention away from the crow's feet near our eyes and we are almost done! Got a fun little purse that just barely holds the iPhone, keys, lip-gloss and money? Check. Shoes that our swollen feet barely fit into? Check. Now walk. Umm . . . no - try and walk upright so as not to look like we are in excruciating pain. Yes. That's better. We're ready to go.

Don't panic throughout the night if you start getting sharp, gas-like pains in your abdomen. That's just the Spanx causing the belly region extreme discomfort. Once we get home and take those contraptions off, we'll eventually get all of that air out and experience some relief. For now, just be happy knowing that it's doing its job - we may even feel like we have enough gas built up to send us sailing through the air back to our homes, but we'll look spectacular while we're suffering. Here's another thing to keep in mind . . . every other girl at the table went through something very similar to get out of the house for this little get together so they aren't going to notice any imperfections, because they are too worried about their own appearance to even care.

So if you're a cougar-in-waiting, or just turned 40, or 40 and then some - let's make a deal to embrace our beauty and have fun with it. We're all in this thing together - and unless we have a team of beauty and style experts following us around, we are all going to have to deal with putting a little work into looking spectacular. And why not? You only turn 40 once. *Raaaawr.*

On second thought, I'm thinking one party is enough. I'm already exhausted.

Andrea is one of the leading experts in the field of mediocrity in Domestic Engineering. With minimal awards won for her blog entitled <u>The Underachiever's Guide to Being a Domestic Goddess</u>, *she has proven that not only does she not have a knack for writing, but she falls short in many other categories in life as well. She currently works in her family's engineering business, is a mother of three funny little boys, and wife to Mark — her knight in shining armor. They live in the Lakes Region of New Hampshire where their days are filled with giggles, Legos, and an endless supply of Greek food. When she is not pretending to work, begrudgingly cleaning up urine from in and around the toilet, or dutifully cooking for an army, she gives her extra time to two local charities that provide clothing and personal hygiene supplies to underprivileged children. Her favorite mottos are "Be Grateful for What You Have, Be Mindful of Those Who Don't" and "Don't Sh*t Where You Eat." Favorite movies include* Moonstruck, My Big Fat Greek Wedding, *and* Sixteen Candles. *Her hobbies included but are not limited to: sleeping, eating, laughing, and eating some more. She'd like to say she is an up and coming author on the* New York Times *Bestseller's List, but that would simply be untrue.*

The Poop Diaries
By Amy Bozza
My Real Life

When my daughter was born, in 2001, the hospital nursery filled out a chart that they called "The Stool and Wetness Chart." I continued this crappy chart at home for three months...but I'm getting ahead of myself. The nurses filled it out while she was with them, and they had us complete the chart while she was hanging out in my room, and I made sure that every single bodily function was well-documented.

You can imagine the horror...not only is every new mom asked to breastfeed, (and if you aren't doing it right, be prepared to have your breasts manhandled by every single hospital employee), hold the baby's head correctly so as not to, you know, kill it, not drop him or her (again, to avoid imminent murder of which every new mom is afraid), change the baby, bathe the baby, learn what each cry means, but also keep a poop diary?! Well of course I did...

When they sent us home, my normal controlling, anal nature had me continuing to fill in the chart. After three hours of being home with the new baby, my controlling nature combined with my out of control hormones took it a step further and I created an Excel spreadsheet to continue to document her habits. I attended every doctor appointment, print out in hand, to prove to the doctor (and convince myself) that, not only was my daughter doing exactly what her brilliant little self was supposed to do, but that I was a fully responsible mother who could definitely be trusted with the life of another.

This all went just fine until she was around three months old. My charts started to show a strange trend. My perfect daughter was only pooping once a week, and always on a Friday. This was not perfect. This was not normal. How could this be? I had been doing everything right and something was wrong. I started to panic, and did the worst thing possible: hit the internet. I know better, but I couldn't help myself, and after reading up on digestive issues in infants, I arrived at her three month check-up, spreadsheets and internet articles in hand, ready to hear the worst.

The doctor palpated her stomach, tickled her, listened to her bowels, looked her in the eyes and said, "You're a little weird, aren't you?"

Um...weird? What kind of ass calls a baby "weird" in front of the new mother? I gave him "the eye" (which I had been practicing throughout my pregnancy, because all mothers have to master "the eye") and said, "Excuse me?"

He tickled her some more, making her laugh and making me want to punch him, and said, "Yes...it's a little weird. But, she's fine." Then he assured me that her body just must be processing the breast milk a little more slowly than usual, and unless it went beyond ten days or she became uncomfortable, I shouldn't worry.

Don't worry. Yes. Brilliant advice for a first-time mother.

Shouldn't we run tests? What about Irritable Bowel Syndrome? Tumors in her intestines? Food allergies? I waved my print-outs in his face and demanded he do more than tickle her stomach. I read it on the internet. It must be the truth!

Sometimes, I wish I had become a parent before the dawn of the internet. It must have been so much simpler then. You had to take your doctor's word for whatever it was that was wrong with your child. He was the expert. Who else were you going to ask? Your neighbor? Parenting in the age of the internet brings on its own psychosis, for which the sole symptom is Googling every cough, sneeze and bit of mucous that exits your child's body, and believing every single article you read, written by nameless, faceless contributors who no more have medical licenses than the kid who thinks you didn't see him pick his nose before he scoops out your popcorn at the movie theater.

After nodding at my "research," in his extra calm way, which I am sure is a psychological trick they teach in med school to make us non-medical types feel stupid, he told me she was fine, again, and sent me on my way.

A few weeks after her three month check-up, I didn't need my chart to tell me that we were on day twelve with no poop production, and my baby was starting to complain and twitch her legs around. So, I called the doctor who prescribed a suppository enema.

My horror was evident, and the doctor said "As parents, we often have to do things we don't want to do, but I promise you...this will help."

I begged him to do it himself at the office, but he didn't have time. He said it was something I needed to learn to do, and that it was perfectly natural and I shouldn't worry.

"It's not natural," I responded. "If things were progressing naturally, we wouldn't be having this conversation."

"Sometimes the body needs a little help moving things along," the doctor replied.

"But, I don't know how!" I whined, and then cringed at the sound of my voice actually reaching a pitch that made my dogs ears twitch.

"They have directions printed on the box, Amy."

And with that, he said goodbye and hung up.

Hung. Up.

So, I did what any strong, empowered, capable woman would do.

I called my husband.

"You have to come home," I said. "I can't do this."

"I can't come home. I have meetings all day. You *can* do this," he told me.

I sobbed, I cried, I yelled. He did not come home.

So, I went to the pharmacy, brought home the package and immediately called my mother, who, blessedly, lived five minutes from my house, and was always happy to come over. I didn't exactly tell her what I needed her for, but as a new Grandma, she was on her way before she even hung up.

My Mom arrived and we read the directions. She appeared to be unfazed.

"People do this all the time, honey," my mother said, but I just cried and cried and cried, not wanting to hurt my daughter, yet wanting to take care of the issue. And, let's be honest, being more than a little grossed out by it all.

"She'll hate me forever!" I wailed.

"She'll never remember," my mother countered.

"So it's okay to do awful things to people if they won't remember it?" I responded. "Remind me of that when you develop Alzheimer's!"

She was not amused.

Eventually, I calmed down, realized that I really had no choice in the matter, and we went up to the nursery, followed the directions and waited.

And waited.

And waited.

Finally, I thought that maybe a little movement would do the trick, so I picked her up off of the changing table and started dancing around the room with her. She giggled and laughed and my Mom clapped her hands and we were having a great time. My Mom wanted to hold her, so I passed her off and the fun continued.

Until we heard the first gurgle.

With that sound, my mother's calm instantly disappeared. In her haste not to get pooped on, she literally tossed the baby at me and put her hands up in the air. I barely caught her and raced back to the changing table and plopped her down onto the waiting, open diaper.

I Just Want to Pee Alone

Like a Dairy Queen soft serve machine gone wild, that little body emptied itself and my mother and I began the process of legs up, old diaper out, 1, 2, 3 . . . shift, new diaper under, until we had filled and disposed of five, full diapers.

We kept her on that changing table for another thirty minutes . . . waiting for aftershocks and rumbles that never came. Eventually, we dressed her back up, ventured out of the room, and life went back to normal. She continued to poop, only on the seventh day, but she outgrew it by the time she was six months old. She was kind to her mother and never required another medical intervention to keep things regular, and I've always been very grateful to her for that.

My baby is now twelve and the oldest of four. These days, the only insight I have into anyone's bathroom habits is the daily call of "Mom! The toilet is clogged!" and I kind of like it that way. I'd still do anything that needed to be done in order to ensure the health and safety of my children, but if faced with a similar situation, these days, I think I'd just feed her some prunes.

Amy Bozza, author of the blog, My Real Life, lives in Morristown, NJ with her husband and four children. Amy is a middle school educator, and in her free time, between teaching, changing diapers, writing a blog, and writing an (as yet, unpublished) novel, she can be found developing blueprints for a remodel of the Sistine Chapel, preparing for a double-triathalon, and ice sculpting in the backyard . . . just for fun.

So She Thought She Could Cut Off My Stroller
by Keesha Beckford
Mom's New Stage

We had a bad first encounter - one of those pedestrian collisions that could have led to lifelong friendship or a lifelong prison sentence.

I saw her incoming - approaching the corner northbound as I approached it from the west. I was chatting on the phone, one-hand maneuvering a mid-weight stroller containing my 20-month old and the required toddler accoutreshit, striving to get to an indoor playspace at least a half-hour before closing. She looked well put-together for a Friday morning, rocking high-heeled boots and a short skirt. *Where was she going? Or coming from?* I wondered, not with judgment, but with fascination and a little bit of envy.

Any speculation about her romantic activity past or present was quickly funneled into this one question:

Is this chick going to step her ass in front of my STROLLER?

She sped up and did just that.

"Wow! Some woman just stepped right in front of my stroller!" I said into the phone, loud enough to be overheard.

Tossing her mane of shiny black hair, she turned around and snapped, "Why should I stop for your stroller? And you're on the phone!"

Oh no she di'int?! And what did being on the phone have to do with it? Had I been stirring risotto while performing open-heart surgery, I could have understood. And when else besides while driving or strolling was I supposed to make phone calls with my

51

kids around - unless I wanted to tie them up and tape their mouths?

I stared after her, my head desperately searching for a knockout reply. Nothing. So, resisting the urge to tackle her and slap her face back and forth in a manner that would be studied by fighting coaches and pimps alike, I slunk off and bitched about my slight to my mom pal on the other line.

Long afterward I stewed. I seethed. And then it hit me. Of course! She was a cute 20-something, presumably without kids.

She genuinely didn't *know*.

She saw me and waved me off like a dog fart. Which is exactly what I would have done to some mom when I was 20-something. Because when I was younger I wanted a life like the Fab Four on the early seasons of *Sex and the City*. But now I was 40.

Like my formerly perky boobs, my priorities had shifted.

Unlike 15 years ago, my wardrobe is now for practical purposes. I am the proud owner of a dresser full of Garanimals for women. Some may see my closet as a fashion cemetery, but so be it – I can get dressed in under 60 seconds flat. This is a key when you have young children who need you for everything - who if left alone might maim each other, or transform your home into a NYC subway station circa 1978. Once upon a time, I had enviably groomed hands and feet. Now there are truffle-seeking pigs with better nails. And as for the body hair situation, I look like the love child of Burt Reynolds and a Geico caveman. But with the help of the few great outfits I hold in reserve, and the handiwork of a few aestheticians skilled enough to transform me from Bearded Lady to Halle Berry's third cousin once removed, I do look pretty fierce when I get dolled up.

In my youth, all this spiffing up was for my own satisfaction, but it was also for sex. In my 20s, I was busy cultivating a rich sex life, one that I thought would be mine for ever, maturing like a fine wine, instead of rotting like an egg salad sandwich left in the sun. These days my level of chastity makes Abby Cadabby look like a muppet-chasing whore. What I want to cultivate now is some sleep. I'm no longer, "Girrrrrl, I need a disco nap so I can get my party on" tired, I'm "let me sleep until 2027" tired. Mattress gymnastics means flipping and tickling and making human burritos in the sheets. With my kids, that is.

It has nothing to do with getting my freak on.

To a cute 20-something, all this seems like throwing in the towel instead of a conscious choice. But it is. I choose to focus on being the best mom possible to the children who sit in that stroller. I am no longer all about mani-pedis and waxes, or fancy shoes and bags and coats. Sure, I still like those things, I really do, but they don't define me, or my life as they once did. I buy super cute clothes for my kids, and treat myself to new things on the birthday of President Rutherford B. Hayes. My priorities - my identity - right now are all about this stroller – this tricked out with Bundle Mes, cupholders, Mommy Hooks, and a colossal diaper bag stroller. If you offend it you offend me, which puts both of us in a bad situation. Your hormones after giving birth go batshit crazy. Mama Bear rage is potent and real. When I'm angry I make Maximus Decimus Meridius look like Barney.

So, all you super cute 20-somethings out there, next time you have the opportunity to show even the most frumptastic mom some kindness, some compassion, some common decency, please, for the love of God, do so. This woman is not trying to wield her stroller like a Hummer on Earth Day - she's trying to get through 24 hours with a drop of sanity and dignity left.

In the meantime, do what every blissfully ignorant woman does pre-kids. Go ahead and tell yourself that when you're a mom, you'll never let yourself go - you'll NEVER look like a refugee from the human race. Bow down and swear on a physio-ball that you'll exercise regularly, wear stylish clothes and maintain a sex-life worthy of the love montage in a romantic comedy, if not a soft porn flick. Vow to keep your passions, your hopes, your dreams - yourself in the foreground. Like Ms. Paltrow, believe fervently that taking care of yourself is taking care of your children.

And even though I wish you all the luck in the world, I'm still going to tell you to go buy yourself a bunch of yoga pants. Size L. Just in case.

Formerly a professional dancer, and currently a modern dance teacher/choreographer, Keesha Beckford is the human cyclone behind the blog Mom's New Stage. A multi-tasker from head to toe, she shows mad skills at simultaneously writing, choreographing, perusing the Internet, playing the role of a mother named Joan "Kumbaya" Crawford, and overcooking food. Among her saviors in life are gummy bears and select cuts of pants from a store that rhymes with "rururemon." She thanks her wonderful husband and her two beautiful children for their love and support, and, of course, for their ever-present inspiration.

The Treachery of Toys
By Alicia
Naps Happen

"I is for IGLOO!" announces an overly enthusiastic man's voice from the coffee table, waking me from my precious 20 minute nap. I groan and bury my face in the couch pillow again.

Then, just as I am drifting back to sleep, I hear *"O is for OLIVE!"*

Putting the pieces back in my son's talking puzzle is of no use. There are a few that have been knocked into awkward places, such as under the china cabinet. One or two have been carried up-stairs or thrown over the railing into the finished basement. I will never be able to replace every empty letter in the puzzle. It will continue taunting me as I desperately try to sleep.

The puzzle is not the only nemesis I find in my own living room. Lurking forever in my path seems to be the musical drum, which seems to have only a "loud" switch and plays a variety of oddly Caribbean-influenced tunes. Then there is the equally noisy mu-sical keyboard, which is partially broken and is constantly urging children to "pick up the microphone and sing along!" Never mind that the poor microphone is now incapable of emitting anything but static, ruining all the fun. But the worst . . . the toy that we fi-nally stole away from our poor child and "disappeared" into the garage . . . is the V-tech phone. Populated by the most annoying callers in the history of amusement, this phone torments unsus-pecting parents with a song so maniacal that it could well be from a Stephen King fun house.

I Just Want to Pee Alone

Press the buttons on the phone, call your friends, say hello.

Press the buttons on the phone. Ring, ring, HELLOOOOO.

I cannot think of anything that will entice me to readmit that phone to my dwelling.

We didn't plan things this way, you understand. When our son was born, two years ago, we actively pushed back against well-meaning offers from friends and parents to loan or give this or that toy. From the beginning, my husband and I had agreed that houses filled with plastic toys utterly depressed us, and that we would valiantly fight to keep our own house in a civilized state. To be fair, we did a pretty good job of this until William's first birthday, resisting suggestions that we buy any number of huge, plastic pieces of baby equipment, such as Exersaucers and extra travel swings.

On William's first birthday, however, we lost control. Well, we didn't, but those around us did. Seemingly unable to contain themselves any longer, friends and relatives bombarded William with plastic ride-on trucks, walkers, musical trains, and hard hats. Within days, it seemed our living room had become an outlet for Toys 'R Us. Each day, William would drag out the toys and leave them littered across the floor. Each night we would dutifully put them all away. We resisted the urge to get a toy box, committing instead to keeping the toys contained in two small canvas cubes we had bought at Target. When the toys overflowed the cubes, we made sure some were redistributed upstairs or packed away.

"W is for WATERMELON! W . . . W . . . W . . . WATERMELON!" the stupid puzzle yells at me.

One of his deceptively adorable toys is the all-wooden walker. It has a row of brightly-painted crocodiles over the wheels that energetically snap their mouths open and closed as he pushes it, getting faster as the walker picks up speed. This toy has become known in our house as "The Clacker," and William has a cruel habit of operating it starting the minute he realizes you have begun talking on the phone. You can walk anywhere you want and he will follow you at a good clip, bringing his deafening reptiles with him. However, the minute you hang up, he will abandon the toy and walk off to snooze with his blankie.

"P is for PRETZEL!" Oh be quiet! I just want to sleep!

These large toys were bad enough, but then came the Legos and the pop beads. Mind you, these were the most insidious of all the toys. Seemingly harmless in their clear, plastic containers, these classic friends of childhood became a jolly minefield when released into the open. William showed a particular talent for smacking these bits and pieces to every possible corner of the room in a matter of seconds. But they were not just in the corners – they covered every available spot on the floor and lurked evilly in our paths wherever we went, giving us bruises with their sharp red and blue corners. Sometimes I would pack the beads and Legos away, but William would get into the closet and plaintively beg me to reopen them. There was no remedying the situation. I had to learn to live in harmony with these small invaders.

At a certain point, I couldn't even pick up the toys each evening anymore. Every two days or so, my husband or I would have the energy to dump everything back in its container, put all the farm animals in their appointed slots, and even get the puzzle pieces back into their holes. But these efforts were instantly destroyed in the morning, when William would pick up the aforementioned containers, dump them out, and throw himself into the pile of toys, scattering them like he was making a snow angel. I had to steel myself against these moments. There just seemed to be no way I could keep my house clean anymore.

Sometimes, when a service person or a delivery guy comes to the door, I am keenly aware of what my house must look like, with toys everywhere and a peanut-butter-besmeared toddler cackling in the background. I hope that other people don't find my house as depressing as I imagine it must be. As for me, I have become reluctantly accepting of the chaos. I make this sacrifice on the uncompromisingly cheery altar of childhood.

"*S is for SSSSTAR!*" the puzzle chortles with delight. I can almost see the actor who recorded the voice, doing jazz hands in my head. William claps his jam-covered paws happily and lumbers over to the puzzle to put the "S" back in. I may have lost control, but he is the all-powerful master of his own little universe.

Alicia is best known for her blog Naps Happen, where she curates an ever-expanding selection of hilarious children's nap photos. Proving the popularity of a good snooze, her blog has been featured online in publications such as The Huffington Post and Parade and on parenting websites, including Babble, Babycenter, and Nickmom and she also was voted into the Circle of Moms Top 25 Funny Mom Blogs in 2011 and 2012. When she's not blogging, Alicia spends her time wrangling two small boys and teaching college writing in the suburbs of Washington D.C.

What You Mock, You Become
By Johi Kokjohn-Wagner
Confessions of a Corn Fed Girl

Often I find myself in a state of mental disarray, pondering the deeper meaning of the Universe. I pose mind blowing questions like, "Why *is* cheese so delicious?," "Is Satan related to the person that invented roller-skates?," and "Are reincarnation and karma really real? Like, really? Fer reals?"

The answer is always the same, "I dunno. Google that shiz." Then instead of looking up my answers on the Internetz, I get distracted by cat videos on YouTube and get sucked into the fascinating dinners of my Facebook friends. Yet, as I go through my life I cannot deny the constant underlying sense of deja vu. There's this chronic tugging of wonderment. I think I may have been here before. Have I already done this? I feel like I've met this person in the past. I'm pretty sure that I mocked this exact circumstance that is now happening. HOW CAN THIS BE? Now, I can't be sure if this is a side effect of a botched reincarnation where my memory wasn't fully erased or if it's merely a repercussion of all the alcohol I guzzled in my twenties.

Nonetheless, it occurs on a regular basis. This is the main reason for my fear-based existence, my curiosity of karma, and my extensive collection of air sickness bags.

For example, I recall a time that I secretly made fun of some truly remarkable back fat oozing over the waistband of the girl sitting in front of me on the bleachers at a high school basketball game. Like magic, two babies later, suddenly I am the disgruntled owner of my very own, custom-designed muffin top complete with back-side chillax-ide.

Then there was that horrible girl in high school. What she lacked in personality, she made up for in pimples. She was awful in so many ways, truly mean-spirited and I was something of a farm-raised vigilante and ruthless with my words, specifically the ones describing her zitty face. Then college happened in a haze of beer and pizza. My face began to strongly resemble the latter.

There was also the incident when my boss and I were mercilessly mocking the apparently dazed/sedated woman who walked into our store with her tank top pushed up over her boob. She looked heavily medicated and hardly missed a mouth breathing beat when she somehow noticed that her breast was exposed. She slowly pulled her top back down into place without changing her sluggish pace, the dulled expression on her face, or the slanted tilt of her seemingly empty head. Later, when I was nursing my babies, the same thing happened to me. Except I wasn't mouth breathing. No, I don't do that. Instead I *married* a mouth breather and our oldest spawn inherited that trait from his paternal side. Good thing that I never made fun of mouth breathers . . . all the time in my college classes, particularly lectures.

Then there are those annoying people who only talk about their pets. "OMG! Fluffy is the cutest cat evah! You should have seen what he just did with . . . blah, blah, blah." Guess what pet lover? *No one* gives a fuck. I knew this, yet I still chattered incessantly to any friend (who had the bad judgment to answer my phone call) all about the precious and hilarious things done by my glorious furkids. This is when I knew that I needed to birth a furless human baby. At least talking about an actual person, one that you incubated in your belly, is understandable and marginally more socially acceptable. Stop anthropomorphizing your pets, people! They lick their own asses, roll in decaying carcasses and eat feces. *They are not human.* "Oh mah gah, did I ever tell you about my horse that LOVED having his picture taken? He was totally a movie star in a former life! And I think my old cat used to be a past life lover/stalker. He slept on my face and always watched me undress. Mew."

Anyhoo . . .

Don't even get me started on all the parents that I have judged. Those mindless breeders who would let their children run feral in public and climb into clothing racks at stores with sticky fingers and dirty faces - ugh! The distracted brat hatchers who couldn't keep on point for a simple telephone call but would turn, converse with Junior about *Dora the Explorer* and her insidious backpack, and leave you to twiddle your thumbs. The unconscious procreators, with their uninvited spawn in tow, chatting, and boozing it up at a party, while their offspring torment guests like tiny tornadoes of terror. I was infuriated by those people. I judged them. I ranted about them.

Then I birthed two boys, transformed myself into a stay at home mom, lost my identity, and now *I currently am one of those people*. Let me just say, **I am sorry**. And I too have been bamboozled by a tyrannical toddler with the ego of Charlie Sheen and the temper of The Hulk. I am constantly so derailed I think my "give a shit" is now permanently broken. Where's the booze? Seriously, I apologize to all of you - except those of you who willingly eat your own placenta. There are only a few things that separate us from the animals as it is, and you people aren't helping. Not one bit.

When I was in my awkward tween years, I obsessed over John Hughes films. I watched *Sixteen Candles* so many times that I could recite the dialogue of the movie verbatim. This was in no way irritating to anyone around me, I'm certain. This was also why I am not at all surprised that my second child is fanatically devoted to the movie *Cars 2* and demands to watch it every day.

I Just Want to Pee Alone

Every. Damned. Day. *Kachow!*

What about all of those people that I have laughed at for falling down in public? Good thing that I've *never* done that . . .

And then there are all the people that I meet and we form such instant bonds, like we have already known each other for years and we are simply reuniting. These also happen to be the same people that laugh at me when I fall down in public. They also enable my foul mouth, penchant for liquor, and love of inappropriate conversation. "You smell familiar."

I truly don't know if all of these happenings are simply coincidental or if they add up to reincarnation, karma and the universal laws of attraction. What I do know is that I am going to start slinging a shit ton of judgments toward every thin, porcelain complexioned, graceful, happy, self-made, rich, successful, cultured person who travels the world with their silently nasal breathing husbands, well-mannered children and their perfectly straight, white, original teeth. The very same that are living in their *Architectural Digest* homes stocked with wine cellars, super nannies, and live-in masseuses. They must be mocked; for they are clearly a bunch of freaking idiots.

Confessions of a Corn Fed Girl

Johi is a typical farm raised Iowa broad. She drives a big truck, scoops manure, adores nature, loves sushi, cusses like a sailor, and rocks high heels. She married a handsome remodeler much nicer than herself, and together they produced two adorable, very high-energy, extremely loud boys. Johi can be found making fun of Wal-Mart shoppers while shopping at Wal-Mart, cracking inappropriate jokes on the playground, drinking wine from a box, and laughing at life. She spends a great deal of time cleaning a house that is never quite clean and trying desperately to find her lost identity that was never quite developed. She is a writer, an illustrator, a photographer, a decorator, a commentator, and a connoisseur of bad TV. She currently resides in a half-remodeled house Fort Collins, Colorado. You can read more of Johi on her blog Confessions of a Corn Fed Girl.

The Big Reveal
By Jessica Watson
Four Plus an Angel

I spent eight years as a single mom to one daughter. This time will forever be looked back on as the days pants were not necessary indoors, the bathroom door was never closed, and I had no one to blame for not taking out the garbage.

As stressful as being the sole caregiver can be, I really did love having one-on-one time with my daughter and foolishly thought that some of the things I had not explained about womanhood need not be addressed. Surely she had noticed the differences in my 20-something body and her own and would ask me questions if she had them. For my part, I avidly avoided the use of the word "vagina," told her the boob fairy would visit when she was older and put a great deal of effort into avoiding any and all embarrassing topics of discussion.

One morning while taking the typical open-bathroom-door-shower, my never quiet or patient ball of energy of a first grader charged past the sink. Pulling open the shower curtain she demanded the latest on her list of questions that must be answered right. That. Moment. Only to stop mid-word as her eyes darted downwards. Praying to every absentminded mother that had ever showered before me, I willed her to ask me about our new soap or my belly button. Instead, she pointed accusingly, her wide eyes demanding an answer, "Where did you get those furry underwear?"

"What honey? What are you talking about?" I stammered, wondering if I could get away with asking about the weather instead. "WHERE DID YOU GET THOSE FURRY UNDERWEAR?" she yelled as she pointed furiously.

I spun around quickly, deciding that I would rather discuss backs than fronts but turning rocked her furry underwear theory to the core.

"Those are NOT furry underwear! Those are not furry underwear!" my daughter yelled as she moved to the other side of the shower to get a look at what her future may hold.

She was still demanding an answer and like the adult that I was, ready to take on any situation, I wrapped myself in the shower curtain and asked her if she wanted to watch *Dora the Explorer*.

My *Dora* trick, promises of an ice cream sundae, and a shopping spree to her favorite toy store did not deter her questions so I was forced to sit down and discuss how I grew my furry underwear and that, yes, someday she would grow her own pair too.

Although I couldn't help but ask, as my daughter was no doubt picturing racks of fur lined up by color and style, that we possibly change the name to fuzzy underwear, or something that made it sound like her mother was a decent groomer.

I still had to land a husband after all.

Jessica Watson is a mom to five, four in her arms and one in her heart. She is a freelance writer for sites such as SheKnows.com and The Huffington Post. *You can also find her wearing her heart on her sleeve at her personal blog* Four Plus an Angel, *over-sharing on Twitter and Facebook, or at Childswork.com where she chronicles life raising a teenager with autism.*

How Moving Made Me Want to Become a Carnie
By Kelley Nettles
Kelley's Break Room

If you ever hear me say that I want to move, please, for the love of Ben Stillington on Felicity, lock me in the attic. (That's all we have in most of Texas where ah'm from, y'all.) If we're up north when you hear me say it, put me in one of those basements (I'd prefer fully finished with wi-fi access, if possible). JUST PUT ME SOME-WHERE UNTIL I SAY IT WAS ALL A BIG, STUPID, ASININE JOKE.

Preparing to sell, negotiating, organizing, cleaning, showing, ne-gotiating, looking, bidding, negotiating, selling, packing, cleaning, moving, looking, bidding, negotiating, cleaning, and everything even remotely related to any of these things, including negotiat-ing, smells like Chris Farley's armpits after his Chippendale SNL skit with Patrick Swayze back in the 90s, especially if it has to be done with kids.

Fortunately, we are now in a house. If we weren't, I wouldn't be typing this little something out right now. No, ma'am! I would be shoving take-out Chinese in my kids' faces with one hand and pulling out my hair with the other. And searching and searching and searching and searching and searching and searching and searching for a house on real estate websites with the other. (Yeah, I have three arms.)

When the whole process began, I was all smiles. I just knew we would sell our house fast and all would be well. We did a lot of painting and repairing and replacing, so what was there to worry about? Take that, real estate market! We would find a house while we tried to sell this house. I needed it go to fast. My kids could only live on the roof for so long before I'd start getting those pesky little letters from the HOA and CPS.

It went within five days.

Well, hallelujah. High fives all around! I'll even give you a high five, neighbor man that sits in his garage shirtless while drinking beer, smoking, not working and staring at every car that drives by your house! (I'm still bitter that he refused to babysit the kids once.)

If I had only known . . .

I won't bore you with all of the hoops we jumped through and the deals we closed and then didn't close and the papers we signed and the annoyed looks we gave to each other and then to our kids and then to our kids again, because, well, you have probably moved before yourself and, on top of all of that, you don't have time for that. I know how this motherhood thing works.

But, before you flip past this chapter, can I just tell you how many times I yelled out, "Are you kidding me?" to my two boys, ages four and eight, during this whole ordeal?

Just days before our house went on the market, my sons and a neighborhood friend decided it would be a great idea to play baseball in our backyard, which was just about the size of your pinky's fingernail.

"HAHAHAHA!!!" my son's friend exclaimed. "You really hit that ball really g—"

Do I really need to describe the crash?

I Just Want to Pee Alone

You can hear it. I know you can. Can you hear the sound of $300 being drained out of our checking account, too? Also, how about my husband's contorted face and glare? And mine? How about the sound of the wet vac sucking up broken glass on our pristine carpet that we had just got all ready to show?

It was an accident, of course. I know that. After my son helped clean up the mess and was lectured about how baseballs have this crazy ability to shatter glass, we continued on our mission to make our house look like we didn't live in it at all. This meant that I had to find a cozy little spot for my son's 5,216 white Storm Troopers that he claims are all absolutely unique and the 432-ton box containing trains, train tracks, train remotes, train people, train track decorations, train bridges, train cargo and, quite possibly, a real life train conductor. (That box was heavy, y'all.)

Finally, the walk-through date arrived! We finally were at the point where the buyer took a look at everything and made sure we didn't decide at the last minute to put crazy clown wallpaper in the half-bathroom, a moat around our suburban house and a permanent statue of Muhammad Ali in the middle of the kitchen. The walk-through was going to happen the very next day. Yay! This is so exci—

What was that?

"Mom! Come look at what [the 4-year-old] did!"

"Did what?" I called out as I was tossing stuffed animals I never, ever, ever wanted to see again in my life in trash bags like a madman.

"Put a hole in the door!"

"Put a hole in the DOOR?! WHAT DOOR??"

The almost-homeowners were to walk-through in less 24 hours. The house had to be perfect. Absolutely perfect.

But there it was - a big, gaping hole in the door of my eight-year-old's closet.

The two boys and a boy in the neighborhood (the same one that was over when my son broke our bedroom window – why did I let him back in our house??) were playing chase in the house, because running at full speed in the house and slamming doors is what any mother would love when preparing a house to show to really picky people. The two older ones shut themselves in the closet and held it tight with their hands so my younger son could not get inside.

He didn't like that at all.

So, the little squirt grabbed his plastic golf club and whacked that door to make his point.

Now I had to fix the door. My husband would have done it, but he was taking care of a million other things at that time and that dingdang door had to be fixed now.

"Hello, Mr. Fix-It-Man. How much would it cost to replace a door and how soon could you do it? We need it to be free and done in under an hour."

He was unable to meet those demands, so it was best to see if I could tackle it. After my panic attack in front of my kids, I decided that surely it wouldn't be that hard to find a white door and swap it out.

Let's just say it probably would have been easier to teach a hedgehog how to sing a Taylor Swift song than it was for me to handle replacing that door. For one thing, the doors don't come already painted. I would have to buy the door, the opening for which I did measure before I left for Lowe's (I sure was proud of that right there), and buy some paint while praying the shade of white I bought out of the 9,521,352 possible choices was the right one. While stressing about it all, I had a conversation with a blue-vested employee at the store and, let me tell you, I was thisclose to putting him in a headlock. We were having some minor disagreements over door sizes. Don't mess with me and my door sizes! I get fired up about door sizes!

As you would expect, I bought the wrong paint and the door hardware didn't line up with the old screw holes. When I finally got the right paint, I realized that the door would have to dry overnight. Ahhhh!!!

Finally, I swapped the doors out with the husband's help and the walk-through went as planned. My prayers must have worked that he wouldn't cancel the whole deal after seeing my thumb prints at the top of the door. (I still don't know how that seller missed my kids on the roof. I had to put them back there after they pulled that little shenanigan.)

That incident just set the mood for the rest of the house hunting experience, I think. When we weren't stuffing our faces at a restaurant (pretty sure I gained 400 pounds during those 6 months, which is why I had to spray all doorways with WD-40 before even attempting to walk through them), we were in public bathrooms. That's it. Those are the only two places we ever were: restaurants and public restrooms. Well, those two places and strangers' houses.

"Mommy, I have to go to the bathroom."

"Ah, dude. We're at someone's house that we don't even know. Can you hold it?"

"I have to go real bad."

"Alright, come on."

So, he went.

And went.

And went.

Knock, knock.

"Dude?"

"It won't flush."

"Are you kidding?"

"No. It won't."

Frantically, I start opening and closing cabinet doors all over the empty house looking for a plunger while our nice real estate lady gave me quizzical looks. All I could find were spider webs and, trust me, spider webs don't help unclog toilets! (I tried.)

I never found one. I was going to have to face the nice real estate lady with the ugly facts.

"I'm sorry to tell you this, but my son went to the restroom in there and it won't flush. There is no plunger in this entire house."

"Well, no one lives here."

"But, couldn't they have at least kept a plunger behind??"

The nice little real estate lady nose scrunched up.

We didn't want that house, anyway.

(No judging. The cleaning lady walked up as we walked out, thank the good Lord.)

We perfected the art of peeing when there was no restroom around during those six months of house hunting. With two boys, a water bottle has come in handy - a lot. They seem to always have to really bad at the really wrong times, like when we are in the car waiting for some house hunting-related something or other and no public restroom is nearby and just letting it all go in the trees is not really an option. (Just don't tell little boys jokes when they're right in the middle of using that water bottle. They tend to lose focus on their aim, if you know what I mean.)

At one point while walking up to house number 4,216 on our journey, we noticed there were a couple of bricks that were cracked in the sidewalk. Throughout our house hunting, we noticed other things, too, like closets so small that a box of matches wouldn't even fit inside them, barking dogs that had ruined the carpets, rooms painted colors we didn't even know existed. My husband, as was his custom, said he didn't like that house. It wasn't "the one for us."

"Will there ever be one for us??" I questioned as I began to wail and gnash my teeth.

At that moment, I contemplated several alternatives to enduring this moving process (that was more complicated than I had ever imagined), such as moving to Calcutta to try my hand at selling woven rugs, becoming a stage sweeper for a traveling Cirque du Soleil show, volunteering as an elephant-poo-picker-upper for a circus or operating a Ferris wheel as a carnie. Any of those would have been more desirable than not agreeing on houses, engaging in bidding wars on properties and . . .

"What are those?" I asked my boys as I stared at red shards ofrock they had bunched up in their hands as we drove away from that house.

"Rocks."

"Those don't look like normal rocks. Where did you get them?"

"From that house."

It clicked.

"Those are the broken bricks from that house's sidewalk! You took the bricks from their sidewalk! You can't to do that, guys!"

My husband made a quick U-turn. We had to try to put the brick puzzles pieces back together before the homeowners returned. We didn't want that house! What could we possibly say to them as we pieced together their front sidewalk? We hate your house but not your sidewalk? We loved your broken sidewalk so much that we tried to take it with us?

The homeowner' SUV whipped into their driveway and opened the garage door as we approached the house.

Goshdarnit.

"Okay, let's wait in the car for a second. As soon as they vanish in-side, run and put those bricks back together! Go as fast as you can and then run back to the car so we can speed away! On your mark, get set...GO!"

I knew that if we were discovered, I sure didn't want it to be me putting a brick jigsaw puzzle together under the homeowner's glare. I don't even like puzzles!

Off my eight-year-old flew with shards of brick in his hands with my four-year-old close behind with his own collection. Pieces fell as they made their way to the little area they had just looted moments before. Their little hands were moving so fast that you would have thought a bomb was going to explode if they didn't put it back together in under five seconds. (Actually, there was going to be one! THE MOM BOMB, youknowwhati'msayin?! Okay, that was terrible.)They collected rogue pieces, put them in their proper place, stood up and ran back to the car like they were mini James Bonds.

SCREEEEEEEEEEEEECH!!!!

If the homeowners saw us, we would have never known. We turned the corner on two left tires, never looked back and then we high fived.

See, the thing is, the whole moving process was NUTS, but I do feel like it brought our family closer together, which is something I wasn't expecting. We may have endured looking at some crazy houses with some crazy yards, a whole other chapter by itself, but we made it through finally!

Now, I just have to unpack these one million boxes. Want to come over?

Kelley's Break Room

Kelley Nettles is a Texas girl and the creator of <u>Kelley's Break Room</u>, a humor blog meant for everyone: mothers, fathers, single women, single men, teenagers, the elderly with good eyesight and highly developed toddlers. She is a Bravo-sponsored blogger and a writer for NickMom. She has contributed to Nickelodeon's Parents Connect and Scary Mommy. In 1999, she married her college flame and has two sons born that were born in 2004 and 2008 that wrestle, roar, and jump from objects every single chance they get. You can find her avoiding laundry and trying to make people laugh on Facebook and Twitter. A lot.

Pregnancy Secrets From the Inner Sanctum
By Tara
You Know it Happens at Your House Too

So, you're pregnant. From the moment you pee on that stick for the first time, you immediately form these pictures in your mind of how perfect this pregnancy and motherhood are going to be. You are going to rock this pregnancy and do everything exactly the way they say to in the books from the get go. You are going to eat right and exercise, you will be strong and refuse the epidural during labor, and once your little bundle of joy arrives, life will be picture perfect. Rainbows and puppies, fluffy clouds and sun-shiny days, unicorns and clean sheets. I'm just gonna tell you right now, forget about it. It's bullshit. All of it.

Once you get over the intimate relationship you had with your toilet for the first three months of your pregnancy, you realize you are hungry. I am not talking just any kind of hungry here. I'm talking about a hunger in which you would eat the ass end of a horse if that is what was on the table. You have a baby in there constantly demanding some womb service and there is no way in hell you can fight the power when you see that cake sitting there begging for you to eat it. Baby wants it, baby gets it. You stuff yourself with the cake and the cheese, and before you know it, you have no regard for what they tell you to avoid in the books and all you want is a nap.

Workout? BAH! This kid is sucking the life out of you and it isn't even on the outside yet.

Sleep and eat, eat and sleep. That kind of schedule makes it difficult to accomplish anything else.

The moment you have been waiting for finally arrives; labor begins and you tell your husband that you think you had better make your way to the hospital. If you are lucky, he will recognize that you aren't just yanking his chain and that this is some serious business. If you are lucky, your husband won't ask you to hold on for an hour while he goes to bale hay. That baby is knocking on your pelvic floor and you are beyond ready to notarize that eviction notice. Pack up your placenta baby, time to move on out.

A few hours of light contractions, a few pushes, and boom. Baby. Isn't that what labor consists of? Oh, you hear horror stories from your friends about hours upon hours of excruciating, make you want to remove your husband's scrotum with your bare hands kind of pain. Not you. Hell no. You are strong like bull. There will be no reason for someone to stick an oversized needle in your back. You are going to rock the hell out of this labor, drug free and glowing. But hey, just so you know, there will be no ticker tape parade in your honor or a big cardboard check for a million dollars in recognition of your bravery if you do refuse the drugs. Just a little friendly reminder to keep your options open, courtesy of yours truly.

Your doctor comes in with a smile. He gives you a good vaginal probing, tells you that you are progressing slower than he would like for you to be, and decides to start you on some Pitocin, AKA "the Devil's elixir," in order to "get things moving." Two hours later you are begging for mercy and yelling at anyone and everyone to GIVE ME THE FUCKING DRUGS! Never fear, no one will think any less of you for this. In all reality, the nurses will be giving you virtual high fives and slaps on your ass, especially when it comes time to push that watermelon sized head out of a hole half its size.

Please trust me when I tell you that when it comes time to deliver that little bundle of joy and your feet are up in those stirrups, you will have absolutely no dignity left. Short of the janitorial staff (who will be in there afterwards), everyone in that hospital will have seen your nether regions and chances are, you won't even care. You now have drugs and are riding the wave to happy town. This pushing bit will be a like taking a good poop and in just a matter of minutes you will be holding your little bambino in your arms. Nothing can go wrong. You are on a Caribbean cruise and are coming into port.

Your doc comes in one more time to see if your door is propped all the way open and while he is elbow deep in your vagina he says to you "this is a bigger baby than I expected". Now would be a good time to start warming up your vocal cords as you will start singing praises to your anesthesiologist. You will be singing and entire opera when you see your lovely doc turn his back to you and whip out a pair of forceps. When you see those torture devices coming toward you, you will start scrambling for words as you inquire as to where exactly where he plans on sticking those big ass salad spoons because you sure as hell don't think that your vagina will be a good fit for tools of that size and shape.

As you try to figure out what exactly is happening down there, you realize that not only do you have a bigger than expected baby trying to escape from your uterus via a very narrow birth canal, but your doc has now shoved large metal spoons upstream and he is now wielding scissors. Wait. *Scissors???* What. In. The. Hell? It is at this exact moment that you realize that your vagina is under a full blown assault from two different people at the same time and there is not a damn thing you can do about it but string together all the curse words you have in your arsenal and let them fly; *Holyshitdamnitalltohellwhatinthefuckdoyouthinkyouaredoingdownthereyousonofabitch!* You are pushing, he is pulling. He's telling you to push harder and you are screaming obscenities while fighting every internal urge to kick him square in the head. Finally, you have a baby. Oh sweet Jesus, the emotions, and the crotch pain, are just more than you can bear.

You cannot wait to get out of that room and take your sweet angel home. You need to get home and get back to your perfect plan. You bent a little with the epidural, but there is no way you can let that happen again. This is going to be just like you see in the magazines and books. Your hair will be perfectly coiffed, your clothes will be clean, and your baby will never cry. What the members of the mommy inner sanctum never told you was that not every baby takes to breastfeeding right away. Not every baby sleeps in four hour shifts every night. Not every vagina bounces right back after the trauma yours has been through.

Before you know it, you haven't showered in days, unless you consider squirting your hoo-ha with an iodine solution a shower. You find yourself delicately walking around your house topless, not for your loving husband's visual enjoyment, but in order to help your nippies heal. Your clothes are covered in poo and spit-up, but since your little love bug often bears a striking resemblance to Regan from *The Exorcist* you decide to test your best yoga pants for absorbency instead of creating more laundry. You quickly figure out that breast milk and baby vomit not only works wonders on your hair, but makes for a fabulous perfume.

When you start to feel like you have failed, like you have completely messed up as a parent, take a long look at that little human that you made. YOU made a person. While the road to get there may have been rough, and at times even unbearable, YOU made a PERSON. While your road may not have been (or will be) this brutal you never know when there will be a bump in the road. Fortunately for us mothers, we are blessed with the ability to forget the painful trauma suffered by our crotch or abdomen (whichever the case may be) and instead turn it into a ridiculously funny story. In the end, it doesn't matter if you caved in and got that epidural. It doesn't matter if you find yourself sitting in the rocking chair for eight hours in a shirt so full of holes that you don't even have to lift it up in order to feed your munchkin. No one is going to send you an award for getting up every morning and fixing your hair and putting on your makeup.

Motherhood is never what we expect it to be, but if you make the most out of it and just roll with the punches, the rewards are better than anything you will ever see in a magazine.

Tara is the mom of 5 young kids, wife to one busy farmer, and the mastermind behind You Know it Happens at Your House Too. *If she ever had free time she would plan a trip to LA to have a quiet dinner and share a bottle of wine with Johnny Depp while discussing average Joe, real life stuff. Until then you can find her on the farm in Kansas wiping noses, vacuuming up Legos, fighting over homework, and French-braiding hair. Doing it all with a smile, a sarcastic comment, the occasional eye-roll, and always with a glass of wine.*

Embarrassment, Thy Name is Motherhood
by Amy
Funny is Family

Motherhood is full of indignities. From the moment I stuck a stick in my urine stream, my life has been one embarrassment after another. After that faint line confirmed my suspicions that I was, in fact, pregnant, I got on the horn to make my first OB appointment. For *six weeks* later. Six weeks?! It might as well have been six years. There is no way I could wait that long for my "official diagnosis." Well, I did wait that long, puking my way through that month and a half.

Since my husband was working on his PhD at the same campus as my OB's office, he planned on meeting me at the appointment. This was a teaching facility, and with my permission, a medical student was there, observing and assisting. That was fine, as long as I didn't know the student (I didn't), and the exam began. My husband was late, and he walked in, coffee in hand, to be greeted by two men standing between my legs, eye level with the good stuff. After an awkward chuckle and introductions, it was time for my first ultrasound. An ultrasound at eight weeks isn't the kind you see in the movies with the gel on the belly. This is a vaginal ultrasound, with a very phallic shaped wand. When my OB busted that thing out, and rolled a condom on it, I lost it. WTF was wrong with all of my friends with kids who never told me about this hilarity? I couldn't wait to tell everyone I knew about my dildo ultrasound. The men in the room didn't think it was as funny as I did, least of all my husband. From his perspective, I *guess* I can understand that. We heard our baby's heartbeat, and saw what looked like a jumble of Play-Doh growing inside me, and the situation became less funny and more emotional.

That experience made it very clear that pregnancy wasn't all sitting in a rocking chair gazing out the window, or letting people make comments like, "You're glowing!" and "Look at you! All belly!" I was a mess. I puked for months, I peed my pants more than once, and on the day of my baby shower, I peed my pants *while* puking. By the time my due date was approaching, I was breathing so heavy I sounded like an asthmatic bulldog, and I was ready to get that baby out.

Labor made that first OB appointment look like an intimate gathering. Multiple medical professionals and several family members crowded around my splayed body, and a video camera was ready to record the entire event for anyone who wasn't on hand to watch the live version. As if anyone would ever settle in with a bowl of popcorn to watch me crap a kid out of my cooter. I didn't even care about the crowd. I didn't really have a "birth plan," but I wouldn't have expected to want anyone but my husband and my mom in the room. My dad stuck around, mostly because I made him, and we needed a cameraman. I showed a dash of modesty by insisting he keep the camera away from the business end, and as you can imagine, he wholeheartedly agreed. My brother and his wife waited in the hallway, but not because they were asked to wait outside. They had politely declined my invitation to front row seats to the big show.

After that, my body was still not my own. When my sweet boy was eleven days old, at a lovely Mother's Day brunch hosted by my brother-in-law and sister-in-law, I showed all of the women in my husband's family how one nipple was WAY bigger than the other. "You guys wanna see something crazy?" Several weeks later, we left the boy for the day to attend our favorite annual beer festival. Mixing beer with my already blurred privacy boundaries resulted in my insisting that everyone give my boobs a finger poke to see how hard they were before I pumped. I loved my short-lived, rock hard stripper boobs and I was sure all of my friends would too. (My husband would like you to know that while most of our friends *did* touch my boobs, it was not as slutty as it sounds, and we aren't "those kind of people.")

I've always had boundary issues. I am an oversharer, much to the dismay of my more private friends and family members, but having a baby took it to a whole new level. As it turns out, this is a good thing.

Kids, by nature, have no boundaries. They don't understand social protocol, so they air dirty laundry with abandon. I now have two children, and they can both speak. That means they can embarrass me. At age two my daughter liked telling people, "Mommy has dog hair on her bagina," and at three she could be heard yelling from the yard, "Mom! Are you still on the potty? Come out here and play with me!" She shares other secrets, too. Recently at our rec center pool she noticed my padded top, and broadcasted loudly, "Oh! Your swimsuit comes with its own boobs!" As you can imagine, she's pretty much solidified my title of Neighborhood Hot Mom.

My five year old boy is only moderately less embarrassing, mostly because he's older - and a boy. The girl talks from morning to night (and in her sleep) and notices things her brother doesn't. He had his time, though. As a baby, he would swiftly pull the blanket I was using to cover his head and my breast, pop off the boob, and look around to see how many people got an eyeful. He would then look me square in the face, and settle back in for the rest of his meal. This year he told Santa that he helped Mommy and Daddy by "picking up lots and lots of beer bottles" at one of my husband's work parties. They both enjoy a running commentary of the size, smell, and duration of my public bathroom bowel movements; and more than once we've emerged from a stall to a group of women suffering from shoulder-shaking laughter.

I Just Want to Pee Alone

Every day is pretty much, "Damn, that was embarrassing. I can't wait to tell everyone." Motherhood is hilarious. And mortifying.

Amy and her husband made two kids, a three-year-old girl and a five-year-old boy. She does not consider herself a housewife, as she owns no pearls and only one apron. Amy is an expert in nothing but laughing at the absurdity of parenting. You can read more of her embarrassing stories on her blog, <u>**Funny is Family**</u>.

A Stranger in the Land of Twigs and Berries
By Suzanne Fleet
Toulouse & Tonic

I'm one of three girls. My poor father was so knee-deep in vaginas when we were growing up, he fashioned a man-cave in a tool shed in our back yard just so he could have a few seconds not dominated by someone else's mood swings.

Dad spoke baseball in a land of ballet classes and butchered Barbie doll hair. He looked at the price tag of designer jeans as if it were listed in Lira. He opened countless drawers to the sound of lipgloss tubes clattering in foreign tongues. And stood at the shelves of our stores bewildered by the difference between slender-regular and regular tampons.

His closets were dominated by once-worn ballet costumes and a shit-ton of Mary Kay make-up my mom never sold. He was so confounded by the exchange rate from dollars to drama that he regularly just handed over his wallet to all of us.

My dad was a stranger in the land of bras and panties.

And now I am a stranger in the land of twigs and berries.

I know from girl stuff. Hair-rollers and glitter. Flower petals and perfume. Hours-long conversations about whether a boy likes you or like-likes you. Growing into your features and losing your baby fat. The agony of PMS and the ecstasy of a new pair of shoes.

This is the language I understand.

But like my father, I've been given children who are completely foreign to me.

When my first son was just a few weeks old, I was chastised by my husband after he found the extensive lint collection the baby and I were unknowingly stowing under the head of his penis. Hubs was flabbergasted to find that I needed step-by-step instruction for the proper cleaning of boy equipment. To which I responded, "How many penises do you think I've cleaned before this one?"

Then there's learning to deal with a small arm-like appendage that shoots urine at you like a six-year-old boy with a super-soaker at the pool. All it takes is a small whoosh of air during a diaper change and that little hose turns on willy-nilly. If you have boys, you must become the fastest diaper changer in the world unless you like the smell of urine in your hair. Although, honestly, just get used to the smell. You can clean until you're yellow in the face, but you'll never get it out of the wallpaper from when he decided to write his name in pee above the toilet tank.

Penises are one thing. Balls are a whole other creature. Cleaning them is like being charged with disinfecting a speed-addled bull-dog that's just rubbed his entire face in a pile of his own shit.

There's an art to pinning a strong, twisty baby boy to the mat while wiping poop out of crevices that seemed to just keep multiplying. But this process can never be perfected because the baby keeps inventing new moves. Last week, a match went to him after he used his new "Kung Fu Alligator Roll" move on me and somehow ended up smudging poop on his own nose. Although honestly, in a case like that, nobody wins.

Speaking of poop, as soon as you find out you're expecting a baby boy, begin gathering information on how to clean dime to quarter

-sized brown stains out of underpants. All of my very scientific research indicates that boys are born with weaker anal muscles than girls. This is the only explanation I can think of for the persistent phenomenon known as *sharting*.

This is just the beginning of a long journey into a testosterone-laden land where confusion will reign. You'll never figure out the subtle differences between villains and pirates. You'll consistently mix up Captain America with Superman, Dr. Freeze with Two-Face. You'll buy plastic swashbuckling swords even though you always said you wouldn't and when they're played with, you will be the bad guy and you will get yours every single time.

Your Lego towers and Lincoln Log forts will never be both structurally sound *and* giant enough. And nine times out of ten, even if you're dressed like Batgirl and twirling fire batons, you'll lose their attention immediately when something with wheels rolls into sight.

Your house will always be filled with the sounds of small men trying to outdo one another and you'll never ever have enough eyes to answer the steadfast calls of "Look at me! Look at me! Look at me!"

Things will CRASH and BAM and KABLAM so often you'll hear those sounds in your sleep and wake to find a boy in a superhero mask standing at the side of your bed.

And now we're to the part where I tell you that I was absolutely sent the children I was meant to have. Two crazy, messy, stinky little men whose chubby arms have placed me upon a pedestal and crowned me Queen of the Land of Twigs and Berries. They love me as only little boys can, which is to say completely, passionately, competitively and sometimes irrationally.

I carried them inside my body and they are a part of me forever.

They occasionally prove this by trying to go back in there. But, of course, neither one will ask for directions.

Suzanne Fleet is a writer and SAHM of two stinky boys who works hard to exercise her family's sense of humor by writing about them on her blog, <u>Toulouse & Tonic</u>. Suzanne's writing has won her numerous runner-up trophies and honorable mentions over the years. Always a bridesmaid, never a bride. Except for that time she was a bride.

The Other Mommy War
By Nicole Leigh Shaw
Ninja Mom Blog

You a breastfeeder? Breast is best, you know. Except when it isn't. Like when you have raging mastitis and breastfeeding is more painful than watching Pauly Shore in his seminal work on the Neanderthal, *Encino Man*.

But, let us not battle over organic versus synthetic nipples. There are so many more important parenting stands to take. There are bigger, more precious soapboxes to perch upon. Like red-shirting your kindergartener or whether it's advisable to let your eight-year-old daughter wear shorts with "Princess" or "Cupcake" emblazoned across the buttocks in sequins.

Truth be told, in my real life I've not seen the traditional Mommy Wars between SAHMs and Working Moms, or over boobs, homeschooling, and artificial colors in foods and beverages. I've never borne witness to a carpool cat fight over iCarly readiness. And though I've seen many a virtual battle on the internet's most accurate and reliable medium for debate—Facebook—I've never personally seen two women throw down over BPA-free sippy cups.

What I have seen and heard and witnessed, both publicly and privately, is the growing phalanxes of mothers lining up on the more-than-one child versus only-child topic. It's not uncommon to find a commenter on social media blasting a mom who claims to shower every day with the incendiary slur, "She must *only* have *one* child." It's not uncommon to be with a group of women, chatting about everything from shopping lists to Tatum Channing's best angle (the shirtless one) while bandying about disparaging comments about singleton mothers.

It's a dirty word these days. Singleton. Moms with more than one kid use it like a failing grade. Sure, you're wearing a coordinated outfit, but *you only have one child*. Sure, you can sign your kids up for five extra-curricular activities because *you only have one child*. Having *one child* is easy. You may as well have a hermit crab or a pet rock.

As a mother of four, I can assert that nothing I've done as a mother was harder than having *only one child*.

My oldest and I were attached by breast, Bjorn, or the crook of my arm for the first three months of her life, and for 20 out of 24 hours per day thereafter until she was one year old. I hadn't spent that much time forced to bond with another human since my college days. We bunked together in close quarters, one of us always drinking too much and heaving it up unceremoniously, and fought over whose turn it is to get a shower. Never mine, it turns out.

Newborn pledging is the domain of freshman mothers, whether you stop at one child or have a dozen more, none are as ridiculously surreal as the first. It's a time marked by scavenger hunts in the middle of the night, this time for pacifiers instead of a sorority mascot, when we do things we never thought we'd stoop to all because we want someone else to really, really like us. The motherhood sorority hazes with sleeplessness, irritability, and an abiding sense that you're screwing it all up. Once you become a sister, you'll never have to pledge again. One kid and you're in.

By comparison, having another child, while logistically difficult to adjust to, forces a mom to loosen her grip on the reins. It forces her to stop obsessing over the health, happiness, and future career opportunities of her oldest child. Now mom has an unscheduler in the house. A fleshy reminder that life rarely goes according to plan and, more importantly, who the hell put mom in charge of everything? When my next child forced my attention away from the needs of my oldest, I was able to enjoy her as a person, not a project.

I realized that I'd gotten busier, but life hadn't gotten harder, in parenting terms. Emotionally, it was eased by the addition of more children. If one wrote on the walls with a Sharpie, I could seethe quietly while whispering "you're mommy's favorite" into the ear of the better-behaved child.

I wonder if mothers of more than one are reluctant to acknowledge this truth because they are afraid to lose their sympathy card. That's the imagined scorecard that parents carry around. Points are award like this:

- One baby equals one point. You're new at this and we all feel sorry for you, but not enough to really help out because we've already lived it and you'll survive, whiner.
- Two babies equal five points because you're really committed to procreation, but not insanely so, and we can offer you help now if only because helping you means we can't babysit for that one friend with five kids. That chick's a lunatic.
- Have twins or higher-order multiples and you get tons of points, but you can only redeem them for help from immediate family or really close friends because no one wants to be responsible for your litter.

- Have more than three, or have more after having multiples, and you're at zero points. Consider yourself quarantined because no one wants to catch your crazy. After all, you should have figured out how babies are made by now, you idiot.

These distinctions, these attempts to put others into parenting worth-categories, are even worse than criticizing a parent over the amount of TV her kid watches, French fries he eats, or Bratz dolls she owns. They are worse because often the size of a family is less about planning and more about circumstance. Many people imagine a life with lots of kids making Goldfish crumbs in the corners of the couch and end up content with one child, by choice or not. Some parents never thought they'd want more than one and the next thing they know they are having a second baby 12 years after the first. Sometimes, like watching a birth plan disintegrate while you labor, the size of your family turns out to be something you have less control over than you expected. Making someone feel reckless for having a handful of children or making someone else feel like they copped out by having one is mean in spirit and meager in compassion.

Recently a friend began a discussion on Facebook with this comment:

"You know how you have one kid and you're all 'This is great! I love my family and my life balance!' and then your husband gets all, 'I feel guilty that she doesn't have siblings' and you're all 'CLOSED FOR BIZ' and then also feel guilty about the siblings and NOW about letting down the husband? Hrmph."

A group of us debated the pros and cons, merits and demerits, laundry and love increases that a second child brings. We related our personal stories about growing up singleton or growing up

Duggar. We volleyed between what's good for the kid and what's good for the parents. I added this:

"We still talk about a fifth. I'm a fence-sitter. But I feel complete as well as completely overwhelmed. I'm working and living a life I love. I'm so much more the person I want to be, and therefore, it's easier to see my kids and my family as a part of my larger life, not a part of me. I'm glad they have each other; but I wish I could give them more. Then I realize the cocktail of circumstances and genetics they've been given is unique and special and not mine to remix. Our children are mine to help and love. That's it. The rest is on them, as it should be.
You have another kid or don't. It changes the cocktail, but you can never know how or whether it's to the detriment or the betterment of all in-volved. If you feel like having another, now or later, go for it. That's on you and your husband. Your daughter is already on her path."

We can't judge ourselves by procreation; it's a measure of nothing more than the result of biology doing its thing. More is simply more because one or twenty, a parent is a parent. If we want to judge other moms, let's pick something important, like how much she spent on her yoga pants or the nitrates in her hot dogs.

Nicole Leigh Shaw consistently wonders, "Why did I come into this room?" Once upon a time she was a mostly serious news journalist, an accidental magazine columnist, and a mediocre editor. Now she funnels an enthusiasm for meeting minimum requirements into her blog, Ninja Mom Blog. With four kids under the age of nine, two of them twins, she lives by the motto: All of my kids are still breathing. Award, please.

Don't Stop Believin'
By Michelle Newman
You're My Favorite Today

When you're pregnant with your first child, people like to tell you how much your life will change. They'll laugh as they warn you about sleep deprivation and colic and engorged breasts. They'll tell you your sex life is over.

You will smile politely and nod your head all the while thinking they must be referring to someone else because you will certainly defy all the stereotypes of new parenting and will birth an angel who will sleep through the night, cry like a kitten only when hungry and breastfeed like a champ. And *of course* you'll still have sex. What else are you going to do when the angel baby is sleeping?

And then you have the baby.

And for the first several months you don't care if you *ever have sex again*.

In fact, if your baby turns out to be an inconsolable night owl who has a serious case of nipple confusion, you make *damn sure of it*.

But much like having clean hair or intelligent conversation or being able to actually see your feet, you get to the point where you kind of miss it, and you tell yourself (and your husband...repeatedly) that soon – *soon* – you won't be so damn tired.

Liar.

As the mom of a teen and a pre-teen, I can now look back on the past seventeen years and see definite patterns in the stages and cycles of parental copulation (and lack thereof) and am here to give it to you straight, because I've lived it. I'm *still* living it. And like any good story, there's a soundtrack.

Turn up the volume; it will drown out your crying.

The infancy years – "Can't Touch This":

Having sex with a baby is tricky, and almost impossible to pull off.

Wait. Hold on. That sounded dangerously disturbing, not to mention illegal. Let me rephrase that.

Having sex with a baby *in the house* is tricky, and almost impossible to pull off.

Sleep-deprivation, hunger, projectile vomiting and crankiness can lead to a serious lack of "hammer time" (and the baby being there doesn't help matters, either). While at first it might seem like having an infant who basically does nothing but lay in a bouncer or swing all day would give you plenty of time to shower, make a nice dinner and take a ride on the bologna pony, the fact that the infant does nothing but scream and suck the life out of you all day makes the thought of lunchmeat, or pony rides, about as appealing as getting a postpartum Brazilian Wax. Plus, you crave sleep so much that you don't want to do *anything* that might put you in this predicament again.

So you don't.

Or you do, but only because you were promised a kick-ass back-rub and a night off from baby duty.

The toddler/pre-school years – "Hit Me with Your Best Shot":

When your child becomes a toddler, your sex life resumes some normalcy. And by 'normalcy', I mean not even *close* to normal. But you might start to remember just how you got into this predicament in the first place.

Because after a few years, when the baby grows up and actually sleeps on occasion, you forget for a moment how tired you've been. Your husband comes home from work (or wherever it is he escapes to every day) and makes you something other than a grilled cheese sandwich for dinner. You shave your legs, dust off the good bra, put on some dried out mascara and remember how much you enjoy playing the grown up version of Chutes & Ladders…for about four minutes.

Because the toddler years are also, unfortunately, the "shutting it down" stage. The years when your child seems to have a sixth sense and a hidden agenda and will, nine out of ten times, scream "MOMMY!" about 30 seconds before your husband was going to.

Shutting. That shit. Down.

The middle years - "Sexy Back":

Just about every Justin Timberlake song I've ever heard could be the soundtrack to these golden years of sexy, reckless abandon. The years you not only remember how, but *why* you got into this predicament in the first place.

Your kids have bedtimes! They sleep! They don't know that Mommy and Daddy's closed door during the day means that they are most definitely *not* taking a nap!

You are rested, washed and groomed (a relative term) and ready to *bring sexy back.*

You and your husband remember the pleasure of each other's clear minds and clean bodies, and the fun of actually being spontaneous. These are the years of the play date, and I'm not talking about the ones you make for your kids.

The teen years – "Our Lips are Sealed":

You might think that by the time your kids get to be pre-teens or teenagers, you and your husband would be livin' large and (taking turns being) in charge.

You'd be wrong.

Much like babies and toddlers, teens don't like to sleep.

Ever.

But even after all these years, *you* still do. You really, *really* do. So because your kids stay up later than you and are totally onto the whole *door being closed* thing, you and your husband find yourselves sneaking around like you're . . . well, teenagers.

It's actually quite impressive the moments you and your husband can find to "reconnect" after a long day, not to mention the locations. It can even be fun in a weird, subterfuge kind of way, and makes it easy to pretend you're in a Bond movie (with Pierce Brosnan, though, not Daniel Craig).

You'd think by this time, you could just say, "Hey, we're going to bed now. Door will be closed. Put on some headphones." I mean, shouldn't they be thrilled that their parents still love each other enough to want to hug naked?

No. *Definitely* no.

Remember how you felt thinking about *your* parents doing it? Gross.

And knowing that your teenager has a firm grasp of sex ed. thanks to the talks you've been having with her since she was eight, as well as just about every magazine in the grocery store check-out lane, it makes what you're doing infinitely more awkward - on both sides of the door. So you hide. And sneak. And make damn sure that when you're taking a ride on the love train, no one blows the whistle.

Listen, while it's true that once you have kids your sex life will never be the same, it's also true that your entire life won't ever be either. Is it harder? Of course. Is it more rewarding? Absolutely. Because with all of the peaks and valleys your sex life goes through in the years after you become a parent, if you can "hold onto that feelin'" that got you there in the first place, it makes all the rest that much more worthwhile.

Michelle Newman wears many hats – wife, mother, maid, cook, vet, therapist and personal assistant to the other three members of her household (a job she doesn't remember applying for). She holds a master's degree in Elementary Education that has been gathering dust in its frame for the past 17 years while she's been making grilled cheese sandwiches and stepping on Barbie shoes. When she's not napping, she writes about her family, the absurdity of celebrity life, and whatever else she can find hidden humor in over at her blog, You're my favorite today.

Potty Training and Prostate Exams
By Stephanie Giese
Binkies and Briefcases

When I became a mom I figured we would have one or two trips to the emergency room over the course of our parenting career. Maybe someone would jump off the playground and sprain a wrist or get hit in the face with a softball. I was not prepared for just how weird emergencies really are when you have children.

The first time we had to take a child to the emergency room was when my oldest was two years old and potty training. My husband and I had gone away for a weekend anniversary trip and left the kids with my mom. She called and told us we should probably come home early because Little Dude was in a lot of pain and might have appendicitis. He was screaming and holding his belly. Of course, we cut our weekend short and came home right away.

We called the doctor and left a message. He heard Little D. screaming and called back right away to confirm that we should take him to the ER. My husband stayed with our younger daughter and I drove him to the hospital.

It was not appendicitis, but we waited for four hours through x-rays, blood work, and physical exams for them to figure out what the problem was: My son needed to poop. He REALLY needed to poop. The stool was so impacted that it was causing colon spasms and had slightly enlarged his prostate.

"Excuse me? My toddler has an enlarged prostate from refusing to poop?"

"Yes, we think so. Here's the name of a pediatric GI specialist. In the meantime, change his diet to include more fats and sugars (to hopefully loosen his stool) and give him the following medications . . . We're going to have to dis-impact him now and then give him a prostate exam."

"How do you do that? OH!"

My poor little man had to have two different doctors invade his very personal space in the same night just so we could get him to poop. And by the way, the smell of impacted feces being vacated is one that will stick in your memory for all eternity.

Then we had to wait three months (THREE MONTHS!) to see a pediatric GI specialist. Apparently those folks are in high demand. We learned that this is actually a really common problem, especially in little boys who are starting to potty train.

In the meantime, we were charged with the task of performing periodic enemas because the kid was still refusing to poop. I had never even seen an enema before, so the first time Little D. needed one I had to call a friend who was in nursing school to come over to help. That is one awkward favor to request, let me tell you.

"Hello?"

"Um…Yeah, hi. It's me. I need a really big favor. Are you free right now?"

"Is everything okay? What do you need?"

"I need you to help me give an enema. Wait, it's not for me. It's for the little guy. I know he's only two. The doctor is the one who recommended it. Yes, we do have latex gloves."

The more we tried to help, the worse it got. He associated pooping with scary doctors sticking their fingers naughty places and hoses in the bathtub and other unpleasantries, so he still refused to poop. The more he refused, the worse it got because he would just continue to get more impacted.

It was a vicious and smelly cycle.

I even took him to therapy.

If you ever find yourself in that situation, good luck finding a licensed therapist for a toddler who refuses to potty train. Most of the professionals I talked to clearly thought I was just another over-protective whack job of a mother and refused to take him on as a patient, but I kept at it because it really was a serious medical problem. I found a local play therapist who was willing to work with such a young child. She gave us a book called "It Hurts When I Poop" about a boy with a similar problem, to read while Little Dude sat on the potty.

Eventually, we got to see the GI guy. Do you know the kind of advice that months of waiting, several hundred dollars, and a third prostate exam for your child will get you?

"He's fine, it's too early to potty train him. Put him back in a diaper."

So we did.

And eventually he was finally potty trainable, at age four and a half.

He still has some problems in that area. For example, there was the time he got impacted while we were living at my in-laws house. He sat on the potty with a lot of pleading and coaxing from my father-in-law and was still REALLY struggling. It was becoming abundantly clear that this was not going to happen without some sort of medical intervention. We knew we were going to have to give him a suppository. My mother-in-law and I both disappeared in different directions, preparing for the worst. We rendezvoused back in the powder room, each of us holding our own bottle of vaginal lubricant.

Great minds think alike?

If I have learned one thing in my motherhood journey thus far, it is this: There is no greater awkwardness in all the world than standing idly by as your mother-in-law compares the vaginal lubricant that you use with her son to the one she uses herself, trying to determine which one will work better on your five-year-old's rear end.

Stephanie Giese is a wife and mother of three who spends her days sticking out like a sore thumb in the middle of Amish country. She might have a badge and educational background that declares her a professional parenting specialist, but her children didn't seem to get the memo. Stephanie's work can be found on her blog, <u>Binkies and Briefcases</u>, *or on her personal website,* <u>stephaniegiese.com</u>.

The Tale of Two Vaginas
By Susan McLean
Divine Secrets of a Domestic Diva

I had a birth plan.

One thing was certain, that plan did not involve two vaginas . . .

Something caused me to wake suddenly in the early morning hours of July 6, 2005. Glancing around the dark room at the still slumbering dogs and my snoring husband, I realized that it must have been my bladder again, so I fought against gravity to pull my swollen body, nearly forty weeks pregnant, out of bed to waddle quickly into the adjacent bathroom.

Sleep hadn't come easily in these final weeks of pregnancy, so it actually took me a moment to realize that the sudden gush was not just one of my bladder's frequent releases, but rather my water had broken - it was finally time to have this baby!

I had wondered what my reaction would be to this moment for so long - would I panic? Could I do this?

Of course I could.

I had been meticulously planning this day for months.

I'm a list maker.

I'm a double-checker.

I was a four year veteran of the Girl Scouts for Christ's sake.

I Just Want to Pee Alone

And I had a birth plan.

Finally in *the* moment, I found myself instructing my husband what bags to put in the car and who to start calling while I paged the doctor from the toilet. The constant gush of fluids surprised and somewhat frightened me, and I half expected to see my belly begin to shrink as I sat there like a virtual Niagara Falls in the first stage of my labor.

It was minutes before a shift change in the maternity ward when we arrived at the hospital an hour or so later, and I literally begged my nurse to start my IV before she left for the morning.

An epidural was absolutely part of my plan, and an IV was one step closer to checking that off the list.

"I know this is my first baby, and my delivery may be a long time away, but please, please, please start my IV so I can get the epidural," I practically cried.

Maybe my nurse had some foresight, or perhaps she was just taking pity on me, but her decision to start my IV instead of handing me over to someone else was something that I will never forget.

She started my line in triage, a doctor confirmed my water did in fact break (you wouldn't need to have an MD after your name to have made that determination), and I was admitted to Labor and Delivery.

Things were going smooth until the contractions kicked into high gear.

I must have asked every nurse, doctor, and janitor that walked past my room for an epidural, and after about an hour of the worst pain I had ever felt, the man of the hour, a tan, bright-toothed anesthesiologist, walked into my room and I felt a wave of relief. Whatever was coming next, I could handle it.

My plan was in motion and everything was as it should be.

After administering my long-awaited medicine, he stayed in the room, scribbling away on my chart. At the same time, a doctor from my Ob/Gyn's office came into see me. My doctor, it turns out, was vacationing in Italy.

How nice.

No need to panic though, I had a plan that I would just have to quickly explain to this other highly qualified medical professional.

"Okay, well, you should know that I told my doctor I wanted an episiotomy," I instructed him as he was nearly elbow deep between my legs examining my cervix. I half expected him to start tickling my tonsils, and I marveled at how little of this visibly in-trusive exam I could actually feel thanks to the magic epidural I had just received.

He nodded as I spoke, and told me that although I was over 6 cm, that we likely had plenty of time before we needed to worry about all the details before quickly leaving the room to attend to another patient.

I was worried that he wasn't being fully attentive, and I also I no-ticed that as he left, he wasn't wearing a watch anymore.

Although his response was not exactly what I wanted to hear, the fact that I still had *plenty* of time, I thought it best to try to rest as much as I could before we got down to business.

The anesthesiologist glanced at his pager and noted that due to the 4th of July holiday just a couple days before, he had a large number of patients coming in for scheduled C-Sections and inductions. "Good thing you were so persistent," he smiled and patted my arm, "otherwise you would have been waiting a long time for your epidural."

About four hours had passed at this point, and the anticipation of becoming a mother did not allow for much of the rest I was hoping to get before my pushing began. It was also about this point that I began to feel really physically uncomfortable.

Assuming I already had a reputation on the floor for being a pain in the ass, which is what comes when you arrive and ask for an epidural before even giving your name, I tried to ignore the enormous pressure I was feeling.

When my nurse, who was both skilled and accommodating came in to check on me, I informed her of the odd feeling of pressure that I was experiencing. Since the doctor had checked me just thirty minutes ago, she first tried adjusting me in the bed stating that sometimes the epidural medication needs to be evened out.

No, that wasn't it.

Did I need to pee perhaps?

Since I was unable to get up, I was given a catheter and the nurse remarked how little was in my bladder.

Better double check my cervix even though the doctor had really just been up there . . .

And there was the baby's head.

Suddenly things felt a little rushed.

The nurse told my husband to grab a leg and since *his plan* was to be at the head of the bed - not the *business* end - he lost most of the color in his face and appeared to lose consciousness for a second.

Were we deviating from the plan?

The nurse called for a doctor - any doctor - and even though she had told me to "push" and "don't worry, with this being your first child, it will probably take an hour," suddenly she's firmly telling me to "stop pushing."

For those of you who have been through a vaginal delivery, once you are there - as in moments from actually passing a human being - there isn't really a way to stop the pushing.

When the young woman came into the room, I thought perhaps she was lost. When the nurse called her "Doctor," I became thoroughly confused.

She appeared to be around twelve years old.

How could she have graduated medical school?

Had she gone through puberty yet?

Forget about delivering a human child, I'm not sure this chick would even know how to put in a tampon yet.

Fuck.

Where was my doctor?

Oh, that's right.

Sipping wine somewhere under the Tuscan sun.

Where was the other doctor from the practice?

Delivering another baby.

In fact, half the of the labor and delivery floor seemed to be delivering babies simultaneously, which left me with a middle-schooler, who had hopefully paid attention in health class, to deliver my first child.

During a quick mental run-down, I knew this was not in the plan.

As the nurse struggled to dress the miniature doctor in the oversized delivery gown, I felt panic set in.

There were several more key pieces of the plan that needed to be laid out for my staff to ensure a smooth and successful delivery.

"I want an episiotomy!" I called out much louder than I had intended.

The young girl dressed as a doctor looked me in the eyes, then at my vagina, then at the nurse, then at my vagina, and finally at my face again and said, "I don't like to do those . . . "

What. The. Hell?

The urge to move this child through the birth canal, my husband's semi-conscious instructions to "Push!" and the female Dr. Doogie Howser standing at the foot of the bed all caused me to let out a primal scream as I pushed with all my might.

Oh my God! Who made that sound? Was that even my voice?

Before I could argue with my pint-sized OB over the episiotomy and whether I wanted to take the chance over a few stitches, I heard the soft, beautiful cries of my son.

In that moment, when both a child and mother are born, the plan, the pain, the twelve year old girl standing in between my legs - none of it mattered.

I paid little attention to the doctor doing the rest of the post-delivery things at the end of the bed, and I just marveled at the beautiful boy the nurses were cleaning up and assessing.

He was perfect.

My vagina, it turns out, was not in great shape.

And by shape, I mean, it surely wasn't shaped like or resembling anything even close to a vagina any longer.

My nurse and the child-doctor exchanged hushed remarks, and by the way the nurse was pointing at the spot between my legs formerly known as my vagina, it almost gave the impression that she was trying to instruct the pre-teen on what to do next.

Another doctor, one of proper age and stature, came in the room next. First, he took a look at the beautiful baby and wished me congratulations. His happy demeanor gave way to a troubled look, however, when his eyes fell on my busted lady parts.

He raised his eyebrows in a manner that both confused and worried me.

"Well, my dear," he began in a sullen voice, "it looks like you had some tearing."

No shit.

"We'll get you stitched up, but you're probably going to have some additional discomfort once we take out the epidural. Just let the nurses know how your pain is, and we'll give you some stool softeners too."

Stool softeners?

I didn't have time to process that before he gave a squeeze to the pretend doctor's shoulder and a *thumbs up* to her before leaving the room.

Was this her first delivery?

Good God!

But God is good. I held my healthy, new son and thanked Him for such a speedy delivery - labor lasting less than five hours and only pushing for 16 minutes - and for my perfect baby boy.

My newborn baby, and my maternal need to get up and feed and care for him is the only thing that kept me moving over the next several days.

Once in my post-partum room, I was informed that I had 17 stitches from end to end.

That's vagina to anus for anyone that may not have fully understood "end to end."

Motherhood was not going to come without a price.

Of course, I knew that from the beginning. I had suffered through weeks of all-day vomiting with hyperemesis, constant trips to the ER, and finally an IV at home until 17 weeks into my pregnancy when my medications finally began to kick in, and I started to keep down food.

In fact, my "morning sickness" was so severe that I threw up every single day until delivery. The medicines, although safe for use during pregnancy, caused constipation as a side effect. This was bothersome during pregnancy, but sitting on the toilet in the hospital with 17 medical sutures being the only thing keeping me from having one giant hole between my legs, and the need to push to go to the bathroom was utterly terrifying.

I had string holding in my insides and I was constipated.

Forget pain medications, I started popping stool softeners like candy.

To make matters worse, every nurse that looked at my traumatized lady parts, would make a sad face or a scowl and then remind me that I needed to have a bowel movement prior to being released from the hospital.

I Just Want to Pee Alone

On my first try, I nearly fell off the toilet, and a nurse had to come in and steady me. "Push!" she encouraged as I felt my humility and pride slide out of me into the toilet . . .

But still no poop.

My night time nurse, who was an older, kind-eyed woman, gently suggested, "You should look at *it*" as she slid me more stool softeners and some fresh water while I lay in bed.

I choked on the water. "Look . . . at what? What do I need to look at?" I coughed knowing full well what she meant.

"You need to see what your stitches look like, in case there's a problem at home," she offered.

I laid with my new baby in my arms for an hour or so after she left the room with the words *"in case there's a problem at home"* stewing in my mind.

The next night I was in a near panic when I finally *had* to poop. My kind-eyed nurse from the night before followed me in the bathroom. I was too afraid to tell her that she didn't need to come in to assist me.

What if I pushed so hard I broke the stitches?

Would my uterus just fall out?

Just when I thought I'd never poop and when I thought all of my humility and pride had left me, I sat on the toilet as the kind-eyed nurse cheered me on as I delivered my food baby while she squirted warm water from a plastic squeeze bottle to try to ease the pain that peeing on my wounds would cause.

"There ya go, sweetie!" she cheered as she squirted my privates with warm, soothing water and I finally went number two. "You can go home now!"

Home sweet home.

Life with a newborn was definitely an adjustment, but I loved getting to know him. All his sounds, the way he smelled, and most of new motherhood I did while sitting on the plethora of giant ice pack maxi pads that the kind-eyed nurse stuffed into my bag when I was discharged.

After two days at home, a visiting nurse came and I told her my pain felt like it was worse in one spot, which she made me point out while laying on my bed.

"You need to look at this," she said, grabbing a hand held mirror from her bag.

"Oh, no!" I protested. "I didn't want to watch him come out, I told them no in the hospital, and it's only been five days, I'm not ready to see *it*."

"Well, you need to look because you seem to have lost a couple stitches, but it's hard to tell with all the swelling," she explained.

I was terrified.

Rightfully so . . .

It looked like roadkill.

I Just Want to Pee Alone

Or like something that lost a fight with a wood chipper . . .

Or like I got hit in the crotch with a meat tenderizer . . .

It was so much worse than I could have ever imagined, and the sight of the trauma was something I'll take to the grave with me.

She let me sob on my bed for a few moments, lamenting the loss of what used to be my vagina before we both took a look together at the missing stitches.

Simultaneously, however, we both came to the same assessment of my crippled crotch.

I hadn't lost any stitches, but rather, my twelve year old doctor seemed to have sewn a stitch right in the middle of my hoo-ha.

It was like to gentleman's stitch gone wrong.

As if I wasn't already lamenting my labia enough, dead center, I had a single stitch creating not one, but two vaginas.

I called my doctor's office right away, but since he was still overseas, I was advised to wait until my six week check up.

So the weeks went by and I settled into motherhood.

We - myself, husband, newborn son, and two vaginas - started to fall into a schedule, and we were happy.

Then came the appointment.

The nurses I had come to know over the course of my pregnancy came to see the baby, and my doctor congratulated me as I laid on the table and we started the exam.

"Well, everything has been great, but the extra vagina was quite a surprise," I casually remarked as I told him my terrible tale.

"Well," he said just as casually, "this is something we can fix right here in the office today." He reached into a drawer and pulled out a needle containing Lidocaine. "First, we need to numb the area," he explained as he began sticking my double-vag with the sharp instrument.

As much as I hated that my crotch resembled the holes on a bowling ball, what came next was much worse. The doctor took a pair of scissors and cut the supposed-to-be-numb-area instantly creating the socially acceptable single vagina.

It was there on the exam table, with my baby in his infant seat, and my doctor holding the scissors victoriously, that I knew next time I needed a better plan . . .

Susan McLean is an award winning blogger and humorist. Her site, <u>*The Divine Secrets of a Domestic Diva*</u>*, has been named one of the Funniest Mom Blogs in 2011 by Parents.com and in 2011 and 2012 by Circle of Moms. Susan's humorous writings have attracted nearly 64,000 Facebook fans as well as major brands and publications. Susan has most recently been featured in* The Huffington Post, *Babble.com,* Delaware Today Magazine, *Circle of Moms,* LA Times, *RealBeauty.com,* Delaware State News, *and more. She has upcoming features in* Redbook.com *as well as* Baby Talk Magazine. *Additionally, Susan was a recent guest on the Dr. Oz Show where he described her as "hilarious" and her "outrageous videos are setting the internet on fire!"*

Susan writes mainly about her life as a stay at home mom to three small children, but also occasionally about her other loves such as bacon and wine. In 2011 she submitted a poem about her love of bacon to the National Pork Board and won a year's supply of pork. In 2012, her Domestic Diva picture won a wine label contest and she was featured on Mad Housewife Wine bottles. In her free time she loves doing laundry.

My Awkward Period
By Rachael Pavlik
RachRiot

You know that time in 1985 when your mom chaperoned the Spring Fling and got on the dance floor during "Wake Me Up Before You Go-Go"? And then she actually *did* the jitterbug? Yeah, she knew it was embarrassing. She did it anyway. Probably because she hadn't eaten a hot meal in a restaurant in 14 years. It's called "payback's a bitch."

Let me explain:

There are lots of little surprises that you encounter after becoming a parent. Things that weren't in the book. Things like, at some point, your little angel is going to throw up and you're going to have to catch it in your bare hands. Oh, and also? Your uterus *might* fall out. Not because of the throw up - they're two separate things. Surprise!

Things that you never saw coming. Things like the aforementioned: You Will Never Eat A Hot Meal In A Restaurant Again. Because once you have a toddler, you will spend the majority of the meal chasing him/her around the restaurant. The other patrons *love* this, by the way. Dinner and a show! When your child gets a little older you will begin The Great American Bathroom Tour. *You mean there is a potty here, too?!* Your child will have to check out every single bathroom within a 50 mile radius. But here's the fun part: they will wait 'til the exact moment your piping-hot food arrives on the table to let you know they need to go. Then, and only then, will they feel the need to pee or even better-- take a massive dump. It must be some kind of Pavlovian response to the sight of the waitress, and you picking up your fork and gazing hungrily at your beautiful piece of salmon. (Okay, fine: bacon burger.)

So there I was with my family in a restaurant and of course Camille uttered those four dreaded words in four-year-old speak: "I. Need. Go. Potty." *Sigh.* Of course she does; she spotted a waitress with a tray. Annoyed, I got up and shuttled her off to the Little Girl's Room. We squeezed into the cramped stall together and I tapped my foot impatiently while she went. Then I decided I should go too, since I was there. Hey, when in Rome. That was my first mistake. I pulled down my pants and sat. I saw it at the same time she did:

My pad. With blood on it.

Now, in my defense I really hadn't been paying too much attention to my lady-cycle since the Current Legal Spouse got the ol' "procedure" from Doctor Snip-Snip. But I knew it might be coming because I had been feeling like hammered shit the day before. So I had put the pad on earlier just as a precaution. Good thing, too. My daughter leaned in for a closer look. I snapped my legs shut, but it was too late. Then came the questions.

Camille: Mama . . . what is that? What is that, Mama? MAMA! WHAT . . .

Me: Shhhhh . . . lower your voice, please.

Everyone knows when a four-year-old "whispers" it's basically their normal voice, but gravelly, like a midget Gilbert Gottfried.

Camille: *What is that? Is that poo poo?* Mama, is that poo poo? MAMA, DID YOU **POO POO YOUR PANTS??**

Me: Ahh, no . . . it's not. It's not poo poo. It's um . . . it's . . . er.

So what was I supposed to do at this point? Tell her it was actually blood and start explaining miracle of menses to my four-year-old in the Applebee's bathroom?

Camille: Did you poo poo in your pants? I saw POO.

Me: Well, no . . . I just. Yes. Yes, I did.

Camille: Yeah, it's poo poo. You just had an accident? IT'S OKAY THAT YOU POO POOED, MAMA- IT WAS AN ACCIDENT. It's okay. We *all* have accidents, Mama. We will just go home and change!

Me: . . .

She was so sweet and reassuring. And **loud.** I didn't know if I wanted to hug her or strangle her. Then she proceeded to undo the latch and start to walk out while I was mid-pee (so she could, I dunno, inform the other stall occupants? Maybe? As if they didn't know - at this point the kitchen staff at the restaurant *next door* knew about it). I pulled my pants up with one hand, fuming, and slammed the stall door back shut with the other. Okay, now I officially wanted to strangle her. We washed up and headed back to the table. But not before she informed the lady at the next sink that her Mama had pooped her pants. But that's okay because it was an accident. Super. I just smiled and shrugged my shoulders and gave her the old "Whaaat? Oh, kids!" face.

Running back to the table, she breathlessly gave everyone there the news as well. Yea. She has a promising career in broadcast journalism, that one.

I Just Want to Pee Alone

That was a few years ago and we laugh about it often. My daughter will be in junior high in seven years. Needless to say, I'm perfecting my jitterbug for her Spring Fling dance.

Payback's a bitch.

Rachael Pavlik is a writer, mother and Pilates avoider. Author of the popular blog, RachRiot, which is beloved by tens of readers. She also writes for Houston Family Magazine *and some say she peaked in high school. She lives in Houston, Texas with her Current Legal Spouse and two above-average children.*

Elite Grocery Moms Club
By Stacey Hatton
Nurse Mommy Laughs

My obsession with grocery stores started at four years-of-age. My parents towed me along one Saturday morning and I was accosted by a drunk, old broad. I've never quite been the same since . . . or at least that's the story I'm sticking with.

According to my parents, my mother had placed me in the front of the cart - not strapped in, of course, because why would a kid swan dive out of a grocery cart back then? We didn't have a lot of money since my parents were younglings. My father was in graduate school and my mother was an elementary school teacher in rural Kansas. Money was tight.

Mother had written out the grocery list on the back of an old envelope from an unpaid bill and was buying only from the list. After all, it was double coupon day so they were going to get their monies worth. Mom tediously scratched off the items in #2 pencil, as Dad placed them in the back of the cart; while the young and absolutely adorable, I sat quietly eating an owl-shaped cookie, decorated with large-grained, orange sugar, awarded to me by the bakery staff each week.

Strolling through the fruit and vegetable aisle, a woman from the opposite direction weaved into our path. She commented on how cute I was, while sputtering and fawning over me, and then insisted on bestowing a gift to my parents' "wonder child."

"A beautiful, ripe orange!" she slurred. Thank goodness I was flattered by the attention and loved any type of gift because if this morning-imbiber had tried this with me now . . . the end result wouldn't have been so pretty.

My father happens to view things similarly as I do. "Too bad she didn't pay for the damn orange first!" said my father with a laugh when retelling the story.

But somehow this soused woman's display of praise and gifting built up my self-esteem. Every time I'm now in the produce section, I'm a little more joyful, a bit extra self-assured, and for some reason . . . craving mimosas!

Now when my first baby was born and I took her to the grocery store, I assumed people would flock to my cart begging to have their pictures taken with my breathtaking beauty. And there was the elderly gifting of groceries which was to ensue as well, so how was I going to find time to actually shop for groceries with all this baby paparazzi?

Needless to say, I was surprised when not every person in the market even *noticed* my child. What was wrong with them? Were they visually impaired? Did I need to prop her up for optimum viewing or did she just need better lighting? *Ooh, pepperoni Hot Pockets!* These were the things I pondered while shopping with my gift from God down the frozen food aisle.

Instead of being a total freak and obsessing about outward appearances, I was the dutiful pediatric nurse (AKA safety expert) and duct taped her car seat to the cart upon each visit. No head injuries were going happen on my shift! I didn't really do this but seriously contemplated it while constructing the perfect jury-rigging system in my crazed-overprotective-post-partum mind.

To further complicate matters, another infant was added to my shopping cart 14 months later. Darling baby number two! And this is when I began my in-depth research grocery store project. I became obsessed with watching other parents and how they handled their children while shopping. I'm not sure if all mothers do this or if I'm just quirky; but I wanted to know why I had lost my "fun" at the grocery store and I needed to fix it STAT.

"I must be doing something wrong. What did the other moms know that I didn't?"

For the next six years, weekly research consumed me: Through toddlerhood when my rugrats wouldn't sit still for longer than their age in minutes, and refused to remain strapped in the cart, I searched for a way to tether my children, which wouldn't warrant a call from the Division of Family Services.

This was also the time when they could strip the paint off the markets walls and the patience from Mother Teresa with their screams for snacks. And as soon as you would give in to their demands, they would hurl it across the aisle like a Ninja throwing star destroying kiosks of kielbasa and kibble.

In Preschool, my daughters acquired new skills how to manipulate others and be deviant at the market. They were proficient at recognizing food items and now had developed the vocabulary to list their demands. Also, having learned which stores had free balloons, cookies, slices of cheese and mechanical pony rides, they manipulated the entire trip. "Who is in charge here?" I asked myself. Dropping my head in shame - clearly it wasn't me with those L-O-U-D, but lovely, children.

Then my day of blissdom arrived when my beauties both were enrolled in full day grade school! Oh, yes I missed them terribly and cried on the first day - blah, blah, blah - but I soon got over it when I first soloed at the market. The clouds parted, the sun shone through and I believe angels sang through the store speakers when those glass doors first parted.

Entering the grocery store sans children after school drop off is grand. What I didn't realize was the whole time I was moaning and trying to quiet my young kids with fruit snacks and Goldfish crackers, there was a subset of mothers tiptoeing in the background – celebrating their freedom, mocking those with poorly behaving tykes, and enjoying every minute of it!

They are the *Elite Grocery Moms Club.*

They drop off the kids at school, head to the store with their grocery list (or shhh, NO list) and enter the store to relax . . . it's a grocery morning spa. Don't forget to get your coffee or tea first, because it's social hour! Many of my favorite stores now have Starbucks in them. I bring in my plastic cup holder which fits smartly onto the cart, so I can leisurely waltz through the store with my beverage of choice and not fumble like those poor other parents who are juggling children, snacks, wet wipes, and Sippy cups. Not this mama - I've joined the *Elite Grocery Moms Club* and there's no going back, Baby!

Go stand by the greeting card section and watch who is really reading cards. I have found many members of the club sipping coffee, playing Words With Friends, or texting their BFFs. Having a great time until another mom with youngsters comes by, and then they clam up and pretend as if they are working diligently. You don't want to rub this kind of delight in their face.

My favorite was when I saw a woman park her cart off to the side in an aisle. The school bus had picked up this mama's kids. She was solo! And she was literally planning a full week's worth of meals on the back of her list. I commented on her brilliant idea, and she said, "It's the only time I get complete peace and quiet. I get more work done here at the store!" *Amen, sistah!* I wanted to give her a high-five but didn't want to draw attention from other non-club members.

Maybe that sauced lady who offered me an orange as a child was only discovering her joy. She didn't have any kids with her. Perhaps she was one of the founding members of the *Elite Grocery Moms Club*. They didn't have Starbucks back then, so she brought her flask. She definitely was more joyful than my parents, enjoying her time alone and socializing with the crowd.

There we go again . . . I'm craving a Mimosa!

Stacey Hatton is a former musical theatre starlet and pediatric RN, who turned her love of laughter into her favorite career yet. She is a humor columnist for The Kansas City Star, *published in numerous parenting and health magazines, and recognized by the Erma Bombeck Writers' Workshop. You can find her crazy schemes and circus acts on her award-winning blog,* Nurse Mommy Laughs. *Her humor essays can be found in her new books,* My Funny Major Medical *and* Not Your Mother's Book...on Parenting *(out in April 2013). Stacey is a proud member of the Circle of Moms Top 25 Book Authors Mom "club," for which she is still trying to learn the handshake.*

Babies: As Easy as 1, 2, 3!
By Robyn Welling
Hollow Tree Ventures

I stared blankly out the window, counting my breaths, willing myself to relax even though every nerve in my body felt like it was being gnawed on by rabid habanero peppers.

My husband sat quietly beside me, eyes fixed intently on the road as if his retinas and the asphalt shared an actual physical connection. Or rather, his eyes were on the *shoulder* of the road, which is where he had to drive in order to pass every semi on the highway at 80 miles per hour.

You guessed it - the baby was coming. And not in the same way that I'd thought she was coming two days earlier, when we'd driven this same 90 minute route only to be sent back home after some hydration and a reassuring pat on the knee.

This time I was sitting on a towel, because I wasn't sure which combination of club soda, hydrogen peroxide, and lighter fluid would be required to get amniotic fluid out of the seat upholstery. Though I was an experienced mama, my water hadn't broken at home with my first two pregnancies, nor had the contractions hit me so suddenly. I felt like I'd tripped torso-first into a trash compactor filled with lava - a delightful sensation that hadn't come over me until I was safely under medical supervision the first two times. Instead of wondering with mild concern if those twinges were going to get stronger and closer together, I was already wondering if it was possible to literally go insane from the searing pain of my body attempting to turn itself inside out.

Up until this point, baby #3 had been marvelous. We were lucky enough to get pregnant as soon as we started trying. The pregnancy was a breeze. My water even broke while I was already on the toilet. Easy. Convenient. Tidy. Wishing I'd brought more towels, I couldn't help thinking we were pushing our luck to assume we'd get to the hospital on time.

But we did. Just barely.

Strangely, I don't remember changing into a gown, or answering any questions from the nurses, or hearing the words of loving encouragement from my husband. What I remember most about being in labor at the hospital with my third baby is the corner of the wall-mounted TV in my room.

See, I had an emergency C-section with my first. During labor with my second, they dropped the bombshell that I wouldn't be allowed to have pain meds. So by number three, I had pretty much come to terms with the fact that most important baby-birthing stuff was out of my control. As a result, I had completely given up on preparing for childbirth. I hadn't practiced breathing, I hadn't packed a tennis ball to press into my back during contractions, and I hadn't compiled a Birth Mix on CD of the perfect songs to soothe my soul while trying to scream a baby into the world.

This lack of preparation is how women end up with no Happy Place on which to focus, and instead end up zoning out on the edge of a Samsung flat screen when the pain of childbirth forces their consciousness to leave their bodies.

Later, I realized that the quicker onset of contractions, labor so short I almost gave birth on a freeway off ramp, and my unusual television fixation were just a few of the ways in which my third pregnancy differed from the first two. And I'm not alone - let me break it down, baby by baby.

Interaction with doctors:

Baby #1: You defer to them in almost every regard - after all, they're the experts!

Baby #2: You've gone around this block before and you've done your research. You come equipped with facts and experience, ready to discuss your medical care.

Baby #3: You inform the doctor exactly how things are gonna be, and if she doesn't like it, she can keep her damn hands off your vagina.

The baby shower:

Baby #1: Ooooh, you need everything! Diaper wipe warmer? Yes! Regular stroller, jogging stroller, umbrella stroller? Yes, yes, yes! What the hell is a layette? Better get seven or eight!

Baby #2: Just some onesies, please (to replace the hand-me-downs that had stains magically reappear all over them while they were in storage). And cake. Lots of cake.

Baby #3: You ask the hostess to save the party for after the baby comes, so you'll be able to drink.

Worst fear:

Baby #1: Medical complications

Baby #2: Pooping on the delivery table

Baby #3: The hospital will be out of that pudding you like

Your body:

Baby #1: You can't imagine how you'll ever get your waistline back, but it's all worth it to be able to experience the Miracle of Life.

Baby #2: You never did get your waist back, but it would be nice if this one didn't completely destroy your boobs, too.

Baby #3: You just hope you'll be able to bend over without peeing your pants someday, but as a realist, you haul your muffin top and saggy boobs down to the store to stock up on Poise.

Expectations for meeting the baby:

Baby# 1: It will be a magical moment of instantaneous bonding.

Baby #2: It will mark the beginning of what will grow into a beautiful relationship.

Baby #3: There will be plenty of time for bonding later, but this hospital stay is your last hope for sleep.

I can't imagine what a fourth pregnancy would bring - I can only assume that my uterus would spontaneously combust. But if it didn't, I know from experience that the little baby would be worth all the cervix poking, ruined automobile interiors, and new layers of stretch marks.

Plus, that hospital pudding *is* pretty damn tasty.

I Just Want to Pee Alone

Robyn Welling is a freelance writer and humorist at <u>Hollow Tree Ventures</u>, where she isn't afraid to embarrass herself — and frequently does. She loves sarcasm, wine, beer, other bottled items, long walks on the beach, and her husband. Oh, and her kids are okay, too. Her goals include becoming independently wealthy, followed by world domination and getting her children to clean their rooms. Until then, she'll just fold laundry and write about the shortcuts she takes on her journey to becoming a somewhat passable wife, mother, and human being. If history is any guide, she'll miss the mark entirely.

A Pinterest-Perfect Mom, I am Not
By Anna Sandler
Random Handprints

For those of you lucky enough to be unfamiliar with Pinterest, it is a website that describes itself as a "content sharing service that enables members to 'pin' images, videos and other objects to their pinboard." But in reality, Pinterest is a service that allows ordinary moms to believe that they can be Martha Stewart when, alas, they cannot.

There are those Pinterest-perfect moms, and then there are those of us who are not.

I can still remember that February day when I realized that maybe I was not amongst those specimens of crafting perfection, as I had thought I was.

It was Valentine's Day, and I awoke to the sounds of children at my usual cheerful time of 5:45 am, and by "cheerful" I mean "holy-shit-for-the-love-of-God-I-beg-you not so early."

The kids at least were laughing and having a good time instead of engaging in their usual twilight bicker session. I got out of bed smug in my knowledge that their delighted outbursts were because I had given their doors a *Heart Attack* late last night while they were sleeping, and had then slumbered myself dreaming of the happiness my offspring would feel when they awoke and found this super-fun Valentine's Day surprise. "Look kids!" I'd say, "Your door had a *Heart Attack*!"

What is a *Heart Attack*, you ask? Nothing but a whimsical little treat I found on Pinterest to surprise my kids with on Valentine's Day. To create a *Heart Attack* you just tape a few dozen hearts to your child's bedroom door, each heart boasting a different inspirational phrase. Gems like "I love your smile and you sound just like Taylor Swift when you sing!" and "You pull-off your gold sequin Uggs like a boss!"

The idea is that the kids wake-up, see all the hearts and inspirational sayings, and are filled with glee on Valentine's Day morning, and pretty much every morning ever after for the rest of time. And from the sounds of it, glee was in fact overflowing at my house. Just as I had planned.

Perfect.

I smiled, happily, realizing the hours spent cutting and re-cutting, glittering and gluing – not to mention taping the finished project in a perfect blend of playful asymmetry and more structured color coordination – were indeed worth it.

"Hi kids! Whaddya think? Happy Valentine's Day!" I said in the kind of voice only us Pinterest-perfect moms use. I smiled at them each – my darling girls, ages eight and six, and my sweet, sweet son, age three.

They answered me one by precious one.

First, the eight year old: "Mommy? O . . . M . . . G . . . like what IS THIS? Why did you write all these . . . things? And OMG, there are like HEARTS all over my door. I don't even like hearts! I like peace signs!"

"Uh, yeah sweetie I like *totally* do know you like peace signs, but it's Valentine's Day so that's why the uh hearts."

"But I don't like hearts. Also? *I'm eight*."

"Got it." I said, with a twinge of a voice that did not belong to a Pinterest-perfect Mom.

Moving on, I looked at my sweetheart of a six-year-old.

With the Pinterest-perfect Mom voice fully back on I asked her kindly, "So . . . how much do you just love your door?"

Not to be outdone by her older sister, little sweetie answers:

"I liked my old door."

"But honey? It is your old door. It's totally the same, only better because now it has a lot of really great hearts on it. Look, let's read the purple one with the embossing. This heart says, 'You always eat all your carrots! Yay for healthy eating!'"

"Can I just have my old door?"

"Got it." I said, with a voice that definitely no longer belonged to a Pinterest-perfect Mom. I watched as she started taking down the hearts, muttering something about how her old door didn't have tape residue.

Two kids down, and just one to go.

Surely my sweet, sweet three-year-old was just the child to appreciate and adore his *Heart Attack*.

"Hey buddy! Do you love it or what? How awesome are the hearts on your door?" I beamed down at my beloved son, ready to share this special mother-son moment, grateful for Pinterest for inspiring this clearly-to-be-treasured-forever family memory.

And speak he did.

I Just Want to Pee Alone

"Uh, Mommy?"

"Yes, honey?"

"I don't really read."

"That's true, but I could read them to you! Would you like that? Here, this magenta heart with the sparkles says 'When you go 'vrooom' you sound just like a real truck!'"

"Uh, Mommy? Can I just eat breakfast now?"

"Sure," I said, as I thought to myself that there was no way I was cutting anyone's pancakes in heart-shapes now. And I reminded myself that some moms are meant to be Pinterest-perfect moms, and some – like me – are just meant to be moms.

Anna Sandler is a writer and mom living happily ever after in scenic New Jersey with her charming husband and three delightful children. Anna enjoys crafting and baking with her kids, always with less than Pinterest-perfect results. Anna blogs at Random Handprints and spends way too much time on Facebook, Twitter, and (of course) Pinterest. She is a regular contributor to New Jersey Family Magazine *and* The Huffington Post.

Bubble Baths and Shaved Legs
By Rebecca Gallagher
Frugalista Blog

I'm a happily married woman of two children. My husband and I have been together for 17 years. Shit. Has it been that long? Well, I guess that's a good thing that it's gone pretty quickly.

He's a saint to put up with me. But he can annoy the heck out of me. That's okay, he's pretty good in the sack, so I keep him around. Not only that, he is my children's baby daddy and divorce is pretty expensive, so I just keep putting out and figure he'll stick around too.

But sex is way different now than when we first started dating. I mean, if you're reading this, mom, then I mean when we were first married. Because we didn't conjugate this relationship until we were in the wedding tent, fo' sure.

For reals though. Sex is hot when it's new, but sex that's intimate and safe is kind of hot too. Or just hot enough. Hmm, let me explain.

When trying to impress a man, one will shave their legs and any other parts that need shaving. For me, it's just my armpits and calves. I don't even bother with my thighs or garden area. I'm pale and blond and my hair is pretty sparse. It hasn't stopped my man in the past so I'm good to leave it. And I once shaved the lady garden and the stubble about killed me. That's just wrong.

And no Brazilian for this girl. Nope.

I Just Want to Pee Alone

So early in the relationship, I made such an effort. We were young, we were horny. What fun it was. We frolicked in meadows and did it on sun decks. No we didn't. But still, it was, you know, *fresh*.

Fast forward to present day. If I shower within 48 hours or even brush my teeth, I've made the effort for some nookie. Hubs is tapping this no matter what. He's pretty easy to please. But it's just too much work these days to do much else.

It's like taking a bubble bath.

It used to be worth it to clean the tub, get the candles out, the bath salts, put on some music, get a book or a magazine and just soak forever. Bath time could be a ritual. Heck, we even tried taking baths together. I never really got that though. Trying to reenact the scene from Pretty Woman didn't work. I guess I don't have Julia Roberts' inseam to wrap around my sweetheart.

Seventeen years later, two kids, a mortgage, a couple of pets, and a whole bunch of volunteer crap takes its toll.

Now, if I scrub the bathtub, move all the kid crap and bottles and jars of stuff away from the vicinity of the tub; not to mention the dust and hair that collects in the crevices, I'm so excited to get in the tub to be what? Interrupted by a child? No thanks. The bath water gets too hot and then I'm sweating. I hang one leg over the side of the tub to cool off. Now I'm too cold. Add more hot water. The bubbles are fading.

In walks a child to ask if they can have ice cream. "Don't you have a father?" I ask. "Yeah, he's downstairs watching football." Really? You get your mom from the tub to get you ice cream? I don't get up, of course. And yes, I know, I should lock the door. But I have this weird paranoia that if something happens to me in the bathroom, I might slip and fall, I could faint from the bleach fumes of cleaning the tub beforehand; any of these things could create an emergency situation. If that were to happen, how would anyone get to me in time? A little too paranoid maybe?

So my analogy is this, if you haven't figured it out yet. Middle aged sex is like not bothering to take a bubble bath. I barely clean the tub, the candles are covered in dust and dog hair so don't bother lighting those, and we're too tired to work in a whole lot of foreplay. It's best to just get 'er done and go to sleep. The faster the better, then we don't have to worry about any "interruptions."

This might sound sad to some of you. Especially if you are young- er than 30. But let me tell you, 40 is not the new 20. I am tired, achy, I worry about urinary tract infections, cancer, and heart dis- ease. I do breast exams monthly, I need lots of fiber. I forget things. If hubs and I get a little nookie a couple times a week- then that's great. Life is too busy. So I'm fine with the way it is. I worry about our tax return and 401k. I sure as heck don't need to worry about when to schedule a Brazilian.

Okay, I shave my legs sometimes. And yes, I take baths now and then. But I guess as time marches on, you realize what life is about, and hairless body parts and fancy aromatherapy candles, it is not. It's about a quickie in the sack, and then getting enough sleep in before some loin spawn wakes you up. That's what life is about now.

Rebecca Gallagher is a mother of two that lives in the 'burbs, drives a minivan and attends PTA meetings. Despite her early attempts at a ca- reer of stage and screen, she pretends she is just living her own movie now. Her writings and musings at Frugalista Blog *are her confessions of a middle-aged drama queen.*

Parenting is Taboo
By Bethany Meyer
I Love Them Most When They're Sleeping

What two subjects are taboo? Easy. Politics and religion.

Allow me to add a third . . . parenting.

Unless I'm complimenting someone on her parenting skills, I say nothing. Not a word about her kids. Not so much as a peep about her parenting style. Particularly if I'm involved in a conversation with someone I know is a complete jackass of a parent. I'll make every effort to talk about anything but kids with her. And you should too.

Here's why . . .

Hi, Claire!

Hope you are well! I know this is a busy time of year with the holidays approaching . . . I bet you're looking forward to that trip to the Caribbean over winter break!

Just a head's up . . . my Timmy told me that your Andrew kicked him in PE today. When I asked him about it, he said that Andrew often kicks him. In the shins. He went on to say that Andrew thinks it's funny.

Instead of getting the teacher involved, I figured I'd let you know about it. Maybe you could remind Andrew that friends don't kick friends?

Thanks . . . looking forward to seeing you at book club next week! Bring on the margaritas!!

XOXO, Melinda

Dear Melinda,

This IS a crazy time for me. So much to pack before we go away for vacation. I can barely fit my daily training sessions in! I can't wait to be on that beach with a book in my hand! Listen to me, I shouldn't rub it in . . . you've just had ANOTHER baby, and you're a decade away from sitting on the beach with a book! If only you two lovebirds had the foresight we did to stop at two kids!

Hmm. The kicking you described doesn't sound like Andrew. I'll ask him about it though. Boys will be boys, you know!

Looking forward to book club . . . I'll take my margarita on the rocks, with salt please!

XOXO, Claire

Dear Claire,

I am nursing a baby and trapped in a body that is 50 pounds overweight. You couldn't pay me to put on a bathing suit right now. Especially if I had to sit next to you. You look *amazing*! How do you do it?

Sitting down to read a book? I don't remember what that's like. Sounds divine. I didn't even crack open our book for next week's book club. . . XOXO, Melinda

I Just Want to Pee Alone

Dear Melinda,

I do look damn good, don't I? You'll be back to your fighting weight in no time! Although, what is your fighting weight? I've known you for 3 years, and you've been pregnant, nursing, or postpartum the entire time! But, who needs a waistline, right?

I asked Andrew about the kicking. He said it's a game he and Timmy play, and they both enjoy it. So, there's no reason for me to say anything more to him. It's just two boys having fun. Sweet of you to come to Timmy's rescue though...I was like that with my oldest child too ;-)

XOXO, Claire

Hey Claire,

It seems like I've been pregnant, nursing, or postpartum for almost a decade . . . oh, wait, that's because I have been. It's not exactly what we'd planned. But here we are, and we certainly feel lucky for this house full of kids. Waistlines are overrated. But I'm coming for mine as soon as this baby is finished nursing! Goodbye, maternity clothes. Hello, running sneakers.

Hmmm. Not to harp, but the way Timmy tells it, Andrew's kicking him is not a fun game. At least, it's not fun for Timmy. I looked at his legs when he was in the bath tonight, and he has 4 different bruises on his shins . . . he says those are the places where Andrew kicked him.

We're encouraging Timmy to stick up for himself and let Andrew know that he doesn't like the kicking. If you could reinforce this on your end, we'd appreciate it!

Frozen, no salt!

XO, Melinda

Hi Melinda,

You still put Timmy in the bathtub? Oh, sweetheart, I put a stop to that three years ago! Teach him some responsibility and independence and put him in the shower. He'll be better off for it. Although, I did notice Timmy's fingernails last week when I picked up Andrew from school. Maybe a bath is the only cure for dirt that deep under the nails?

Again, I don't see any reason to correct Andrew about "kicking" Timmy. Your son should take this opportunity to stick up for himself. If he doesn't like Andrew "kicking" him, let him speak up. Fighting his battles for him isn't going to make him independent. Sorry to be the bearer of bad news. SMH

XO, Claire

Claire,

I'm afraid I don't understand what you mean by Timmy's fingernails. Can you elaborate? Their class had art one day last week, so Timmy had clay under his fingernails. Is that what you mean?

I also don't understand why you're placing quotation marks around the word kicking. Are you implying Timmy is lying? Because Jackson's Mom knocked on my window at carline on Tuesday to tell me that Jackson told *her* that Andrew repeatedly kicks Timmy at school. Jackson told her Timmy had cried about it, while Andrew stood and laughed at him. Sounds like a classic case of bullying to me.

I can see the allure of showers. They are easier. No sore knees and aching back from leaning over a tub. No tub toys needing air drying. But Timmy and his younger brother, Kyle, look forward to their baths. It's a nice time for them to play with each other, and I try to get some laundry folded while they are in the bathtub.

We hope our kids grow up to be independent. We want them to learn to stick up for themselves. But, as parents, our job is to be their voice until they can find their own voices. Which is why I'm using my voice to defend my child from your son. SMH right back at you.

Sincerely, Melinda

Melinda,

Let me guess . . . do you also sing to them when they're in the bathtub? You are *so* darling! Really, you are. How is it you have laundry to fold in the evening? I'm surprised you can't get it done when you're home all day. When my kids were young, I managed to get the laundry done during the day. Which was a challenge because I had my daily training sessions, and I played in two *very* competitive tennis leagues. I also pureed all of their baby food from organic fruits, vegetables, and meats. Farm to table is the only way we operate in this house.

This is getting a little bit ridiculous. I propose we meet with the kids to discuss this alleged kicking. It will give Andrew the opportunity to explain himself. And Timmy obviously needs coaxing to stick up for himself.

Who is Jackson's mother? The one who walks around slinging the fake Tory Burch bag? I'd be hesitant to believe anything *her* boy says. Would you really trust a woman who walks around with a flea market knock off draped over her shoulder?

Claire

Claire,

Alleged kicking? I have a memory like an elephant, and I remember Timmy said that Andrew kicked Jackson during the first week of school. There's a pattern of violent behavior with your son. As his mother, you must acknowledge that and make every effort to put an end to it.

Melinda

Melinda,

Make no mistake, Melinda, you have thighs like an elephant. Violent behavior? I realize you're hormones are fluctuating as rapidly as your weight. But, please, do make an effort to simmer down. . . Claire

Claire,

Jackson's Mom said she talked to you about this at pickup. She said you blamed Andrew's kicking on his "restless leg syndrome." Is that even a disease? Sounds more like an after school special.

Maybe you should spend less time questioning the authenticity of someone's designer handbag and keep a closer eye on your daughter. Judging by the outfit she wore to the Boy Scout pinning ceremony, she'll be on the pole before she has her driver's license. Like mother like daughter, right?

It's obvious Andrew gets his mean streak from you. Your husband is a doll. How does that gentle soul of a man put up with your aggressive behavior?

Melinda

Melinda,

My husband has his hands full . . . figuratively . . . with me in the bedroom. Unlike your poor husband. Who has his hands *more* than full . . . literally . . . with you.

Speaking of your husband, I heard he and Owen's Mom have been getting *very* friendly. If you know what I mean . . .

Claire

Claire, That's ironic. Because I heard your husband and Owen's *Dad* have been getting very friendly. If you know what *I* mean . . . Melinda

BOOM!

Now you've done it. Within three minutes, you're down a Facebook friend. You've lost a Twitter follower. Worst of all, she's blocked you from her Pinterest boards. All before you had the chance to pin her legendary cheese ball recipe. Looks like you're bringing yet another veggie tray to book club, girlfriend.

Wait, what's this in your inbox?

Melinda,

We heard you outed Claire's husband. Consider yourself no longer a member of this group.

Signed, Your Ex-Book Club

Ooof.

What subjects are taboo? Religion and politics.
And parenting.

Bethany Meyer lives in Philadelphia, PA, with her husband and their four sons. No, they will not be trying for a girl. Bethany's work has been featured on The Huffington Post. *She loves writing, running, and color-coding her calendar to keep track of her kids' activities. Scratch that. She loves writing on her blog,* I Love Them Most When They are Sleeping, *and running. And her husband and kids.*

The Husbands Who Cried Wolf-itis
By Lisa and Ashley
The Dose of Reality

Let it be known right off the bat, we have initials that go with our full names. Lisa's are M.D. and Ashley's are R.N. You might think that being married to someone in the medical profession would come with certain benefits. Maybe we're like Albert Schweitzer and Florence Nightingale all wrapped up in one, diagnosing their aliments and caring for them with compassion during their man-colds. Surely we're consumed with keeping track of their Motrin dosing schedule and lovingly applying cool compresses to their foreheads.

You might think those things, but you would be wrong.

Because neither of us is involved in patient care on a daily basis anymore, we really enjoy functioning as private WebMDs for our friends. Our fellow moms always come to us with legitimate and normal concerns. We love to help them. But our husbands are another matter. Something about taking our marriage vows eliminated our tolerance for their whining, sniffling, and dramatic over-reactions to their every ache and pain. In fact, we endlessly complain about their latest hypochondriacal maladies to each other. Daily.

Hence our conversation from last Tuesday:

Ashley: Seriously, get ready for the latest complaint from my damn husband. Keep in mind that every. Single. Word. I am about to share with you came directly from his lips.

Lisa: Oh God, I can tell this is going to be good.

Ashley: That man looked at me last night and said, "I am really worried about my knee. It feels really spongy--YES HE SAID THAT VERY WORD-- and loose around my kneecap." I let him know that he is over 40 now and that's going to happen. I told him to get a knee brace from Walgreens, and he'd be good to go.

Lisa: Yep. Total weekend warrior syndrome. That was good advice. Did it reassure him?

Ashley: Ha! No, not even close. He wondered if he should make an appointment with an orthopedist for a custom brace or maybe an MRI.

Lisa: Wow. Just wow.

Ashley: The best part is yet to come. The *next* thing he said to me was (and I quote), "I am really nervous it will just buckle, and I will need emergency knee surgery."

Lisa: Bwahahaha! Oh, Lawd! What is he, a linebacker for the NFL all of the sudden? Which orthopedist do you have on retainer? I wonder if knee buckle surgery is arthroscopic or invasive?

Ashley: I wonder if it's covered under our insurance! I assured him that I was pretty confident he was safe from a dreaded case of "the knee buckle."

Lisa: This must be the week for joint complaints in the over 40 male population.

Ashley: Oh, do tell!

Lisa: My brave little soldier of a husband has decided that he has a raging case of tennis elbow. Except, instead of taking an ibuprofen and going on with his life like a normal person, he thinks it's best to go around the house wincing and moaning every time he tries to pick something up. He has even taken to freezing in mid-motion and crying out in agony.

Ashley: Did you tell him to get a brace? Maybe our husbands can go together. Perhaps they can find a buy-one-get-one-free special or something.

Lisa: Oh, I wish it were that simple. Unfortunately, the over-exaggeration of his "pain" led our sweet, somewhat anxious son to decide that his father was gravely ill. Bobby was so concerned that he took me aside because he was worried his father had somehow contracted elbow cancer.

Ashley: Poor kid! Hey, wait a minute! Don't *you* have tennis elbow from time to time?

Lisa: Why, yes . . . yes I do. In fact, when I tried to commiserate with my dear husband at dinner and offer tips for dealing with it, do you know what he actually said to me?

Ashley: No, but I can't wait to find out.

Lisa: He said, "Oh, that's right. I forgot you had tennis elbow." Um, OF COURSE HE DID because I don't go around complaining about it all of the time.

Ashley: I bet he felt bad then, right?

Lisa: Oh, no! In fact, he had the nerve to say, "My case must be worse than yours. You would not be able to function with pain like this." You will be proud to know I suppressed the urge to stab him with my fork.

Ashley: Bravo, sister. You deserve a medal for that.

Don't judge us. We are caring people.

If you had to put up with the litany of complaints we do on a daily basis, you'd become hardened to their whimpers, too. After years of cases of "malaria" that turn out to be nothing more than a zit, we feel totally justified in our penchant for dismissing their illnesses outright. We have no problem assuring our husbands they won't catch rickets just because they spend all day in an office environment. We feel perfectly comfortable treating their paper cuts with a simple Band-Aid. We are also absolutely positive they won't contract scurvy because we callously refused to buy the imported crate of tangelos they wanted from Harry and David.

As a rule, we are always correct.

But . . . let's just say that *hypothetically* there may have been a time when each of our husbands complained of a severe cough. We might have suggested they suck on a Ricola and relax. Let's just say that they both continued to insist they were getting worse by the second and begged us to listen to their wheezy chests. Maybe we assured them they didn't have the bubonic plague and that, while colds are indeed unpleasant, they are harmless. Let's just say that after they each spent days lounging in bed, we sent them to the doctor so he would tell them to man up. It's *possible* that they both *hypothetically* came home with the official diagnosis of pneumonia.

Boy, did we learn a lesson.

No, that lesson isn't that husband coughs should be taken seriously. Have you even read a single word we've written?

The takeaway is that husbands who cry wolf-itis, only have themselves to blame when we tell them to take two aspirin and call us in the morning. Obviously.

I Just Want to Pee Alone

Lisa and Ashley are the voices behind the blog, <u>The Dose of Reality</u>.

Lisa is a 40-something mother, wife, and in her previous life, she was a practicing physician in Internal Medicine. These days the only doctoring she does is diagnosing her kids with "don't want to go to bed-itis" and assuring her husband that man-colds are not fatal.

Ashley is a mostly-stay-at-home mom, wife, and an occasional nurse (turns out she would rather just play a nurse on TV). At this point, she stands a better chance of creating world peace than keeping her house clean and organized.

Lisa and Ashley feel that if it takes a village, shouldn't that village be honest and hold each other up, rather than knock each other down by pretending we are perfect? At The Dose of Reality, you will get that kind of truth, because they believe strongly in telling it like it is, like it really is.

The Mom-Chauffeur
By Kristen
Life On Peanut Layne

I'm not sure when it happened that I morphed from a mom to a chauffeur. I know those of you with small children are thinking, "Wait, so you mean not only did I get fat and permanently ruin my vagina pushing their giant heads out of my loins, but I have to drive them around too?" Driving kids around is probably one of my least favorite aspects of parenthood. If I had known that I was going to spend three quarters of my adult life trapped inside of a grungy minivan that smells of rotten french fries and assholes (don't ask), I may have thought twice about having five kids.

I'm not a patient person. I have a little thing called road rage. Nothing makes me happier than driving up and down a one lane road at 20 mph with multiple four way stops. People are morons. I don't understand why it's so difficult to gauge who has the right of way? Was there a Cliff's Notes version of the DMV test I wasn't aware of, because I actually read the stupid manual from cover to cover which outlined the order of traffic at a four way stop in great detail. I have flipped many a birds at these four way stops.

Driving the same route every single day has turned me into a drone. Verizon could clone me and make robot mommies with built in GPS systems. It's true. I could drive these routes in my sleep. Sometimes I get to my destination and don't even remember driving there. And no I swear I don't drink. I wouldn't be so angry all the time if I were drunk. The best is when you have to make an extra trip because your middle schooler has Thursday detention again because she gave her PE teacher some sass about not want-ing to ruin her make up so she didn't dress down. Who's freaking child is this I ask? I swear her mom (me) doesn't even know how to apply make up and looks like the grim reaper who lives in one pair of stretched out yoga pants with the butt so stretched out that it looks like I crapped my pants and just left it in there to stew.

So anyways, you find yourself sitting in the carpool line of shame with all the other parents of delinquent children who also have detention and you see your daughter come out with a new friend. You take a deep breath and hope she isn't going to ask you to drive this little darling home. No such luck. As they approach the van, you notice this girl has more grey hair than you do because she dyed it that way on purpose! You quickly reach for your phone to do a Google search to make sure there aren't any new Portland gangs for 13-year-old girls who are purposely trying to look 40, but you don't see anything. Then you hear the dreaded question, "Can you give Ashley a ride home?" You want to scream, "HELL NO" but you don't want to look like the rude selfish asshole that you really are, so you begrudgingly say, "I guess so." Of course her friend lives 15 minutes away in the opposite direction of where you're going and you nearly get sideswiped while playing chicken with oncoming traffic, while almost wiping out the pedestrian that you can't see darting across the crosswalk.

You barely manage to pull into her driveway with your heart beating out of your chest because you just drove in rush hour traffic and the only directions you got from this child were, "Oh yeah, you're going to turn up ahead" as she goes back to smacking her gum and chatting with your daughter in the backseat. Fuck me. As she climbs out of your van, not only does she not properly shut the door all the way so you have to get out and re-close it, but you don't even get a thank you. You memorize her house number so you can come back and kick her parents square in the taco for not teaching their kid any manners.

Life on Peanut Layne

You fight rush hour traffic home almost getting a couple of red light tickets thanks to Portland's awesome red light cameras they have all over the city, pull into your driveway just in time for the empty gas light button to ding on your dashboard. You kick off your shoes and set down your keys when your teenage son calls out, "Hey mom, can you give me a ride to Jordan's?"

Kristen is a SAHM of five and a humorist blogger at **Life On Peanut Layne**. *Her blog's tagline reads: "Providing laughter, entertainment, and permanent birth control to the entire neighborhood" and she's not kidding. Her goal is to make her readers laugh so hard they cry or possibly even lose bladder control. She isn't afraid to write about the embarrassing or uncomfortable things that many people are thinking, but would never actually say out loud.*

Lumps, Hand Mirrors, and Elephants: My Nightmare Down There
By Anna Luther
My Life and Kids

My middle child was eight weeks old when I felt a lump.

Down there.

I felt it for days, in-between breastfeeding and trying to convince my toddler not to hit the baby.

I could feel it growing.

I begged my husband to take a peek, but he was terrified of what he might find. He finally agreed to feel it.

Four years later, and he still hasn't recovered.

I talked to my friends about it. I Googled it. I WebMD'd it.

At best, it was a cyst that would need to be lanced before an infection set in. At worst, it was cancer.

My babysitter cancelled less than an hour before my Ob/Gyn appointment, so I took my 17-month-old and my 2-month-old to the doctor's office with me.

I got undressed.

I sang *Twinkle, Twinkle, Little Star.*

I passed out sippy cups and bottles.I tried not to cry as I waited for the doctor.

When it was time, I nervously scooted to the end of the table and put my legs in the stirrups.

The baby started crying, and I handed my toddler a sucker while the doctor felt the lump.

"Is this what you're feeling?" he asked.

"Yes," I said. "That's it. It's gotten bigger. And it hurts."

"Do you think it's cancer?" I whispered.

I started shaking a little. Tears ran down my face.

"Well," he said, making sure I could hear him over the crying baby.

"That is a pimple."

The baby stopped crying.

I sat up in shock, and the room started spinning a little.

The toddler dropped his sucker.

I alternated feelings of total and utter relief and total and utter embarrassment.

I closed my legs, and the doctor stood up.

"You can always use a hand mirror and take a peek before you come in next time," he said.

Which is how I found myself in my bathroom with a hand mirror - looking at my mutilated vagina less than three months after giving birth to my second child.

I Just Want to Pee Alone

What I saw still gives me nightmares.

There, in the mirror, was the largest, oldest, saddest looking elephant I have ever seen.

And right in the middle of his forehead, was a giant zit.

Anna Luther is the mom behind the blog, <u>My Life and Kids</u>, where she strives to make you feel better about your messy, crazy, fabulous life. She was chosen by Parents Magazine *as one of the top five blogs Most Likely to Make You Laugh. Anna is the mother of three little kids, the driver of a minivan, and the wife of Even Steven. She knows nearly 50 ways to make realistic farting noises.*

The God's Honest Truth About Breastfeeding
By Dani Ryan
Cloudy, With a Chance of Wine

Prior to the time my husband and I decided to pull the goalie and start trying for kids, I never pegged myself as the type that would breastfeed. It's not that I had an issue with it. I just couldn't, for the life of me, envision myself turning into a baby-wearing, breastfeeding mama.

I thought such practices were reserved for hippies.

Like my sister-in-law.

Little did I know I would one day find myself (shamelessly) sitting topless on our living room floor with my boob in my daughter's mouth while arguing the ergonomic superiority of the Ergo Baby Carrier to my husband.

That's right, my friends. I drank the Kool-Aid. I became the mother I swore up and down I would never become. I breastfed my daughter for *11 months*.

But here's the thing: I didn't enjoy it, and I hated how isolated I felt when other women told me how magical their breastfeeding "journey" was, and how sad they were when their child self-weaned at the age of four. It made me feel like an even shittier mother than I already felt when I silently cursed each time I had to drag myself out of bed in the middle of the night to nurse my child back to sleep.

The trouble is, I was so knee-deep in my postpartum misery that I didn't have the balls to admit I'm really not the baby-wearing, breastfeeding type. The good news is, my daughter obviously felt the same way and cut that shit off before someone had to take me away in a straitjacket.

And that *was the magical moment when I looked into her eyes and thought, "It's you and me against the world, baby."*

It's been over a year since my daughter tossed my breasts aside, and now that I've (mostly) regained my sanity, I feel like it's time to take a stand. It's time to hold up my middle finger and yell "Fuck you!" to the breastfeeding gods.

I think I've earned that right.

So here it is, my friends.

The god's honest truth about breastfeeding:

- **It hurts.** Anyone who's breastfed a child will tell you it hurts, but they'll claim it's "hard to describe" and keep it at that. I beg to differ. I think it's pretty easy to describe. Imagine filling one of your husband's testicles with water, stretching it to at least two times its size, taking a razor to the center of it, and then dropping it into a bucket of acid. That's pretty much how it feels to breastfeed your newborn for the first two weeks. And as an added bonus, you will be doing this every 45 to 90 minutes 'round the clock for weeks on end, making those contractions you were yelling about not so long ago seem like nothing but a distant memory.

- **Nipple confusion, schnipple confusion.** All the experts will tell you to exclusively breastfeed for the first 6 to 12 weeks to ensure you don't confuse your child and complicate your breastfeeding relationship. Looking back, I'm pretty sure this whole idea of nipple confusion was dreamed up by a man (I'm talking to you, Dr. Sears), because exclusive breastfeeding means that, regardless of how tired you are or how much pain you are feeling after pushing a baby out of your vagina, there will be no reason for your husband to get up in the middle of the night. Ever. If the baby's hungry, it's all you, my sweets.

- **Not all bottles are created equal.** Other experts (obviously of the female persuasion) will tell you how important it is to introduce a bottle somewhere between the 6 to 12 week mark to ensure your child will take milk from someone else if needed. What they don't tell you is that you need a PhD to decipher which bottle and nipple is best for which kind of baby. And if you're stupid enough to use the bottle that comes with your Medela breast pump like I was, you can expect to spend the next 24 hours pacing your living room while trying to help your precious baby pass gas.

- **It's like show-and-tell.** A lot of women are very blasé about breastfeeding. They do it at the mall, at the park, at a restaurant, even on their couch while visiting with their father-in-law. My hat goes off to them as I could never bring myself to do this. It's not that I think it's wrong. Quite the contrary, actually. It's just that I know from ex-perience that the eye automatically gravitates towards the pink elephant in the room. It's like that woman at the gym who *insists* on talking to me while she's naked - no matter how hard I try to keep my eyes north, I cannot ignore the hip-to-hip mess she has going on down south (how does her husband know where to put it?). The same goes for breastfeeding. While I don't care if you're doing it in front of me, I cannot be trusted not to tell my husband you have nipples the size of dinner plates. Just sayin'.

- **Hooter hiders are useless.** For those who aren't in-the-know, a Hooter Hider is a makeshift apron that allows you to discreetly nurse in public. Turns out this is about as awesome an invention as the Snuggie - not only is it next to impossible to hold a squirming baby while gingerly un-buttoning your top underneath the damn thing without employing the help of a stranger, it also annoys the shit out of most babies over the 10 week mark. Have you ever tried eating with a sheet over your head? I didn't think so.

- **Nursing bras make granny panties look sexy.** Unless your husband wants a shot of breast milk in his mouth every time he makes his O face, it's essential that you keep your nursing bra on while doing the deed. Sadly, nursing bras make my Grandmother's knickers look like something out of a Victoria's Secret catalog, so unless your husband is bordering on legal blindness, I'd keep the mood lighting to a minimum when engaging in adult games during your breastfeeding "journey."

- **Sour milk is the nursing mother's fragrance of choice.** Nursing bras are not only ugly, they're also expensive, so chances are you'll only own three or four of them to begin with. This isn't an issue as your washing machine runs non-stop anyway. But as personal hygiene is often the first thing to slip once sleep deprivation takes its hold, it's only a matter of time before you get used to the smell of sour milk and start wearing your nursing bras past their best before date. This doesn't bode well for you when you're trying to show the world you have your shit together . . . like at your baby's three-month check-up.

- **Beware of the human pacifier.** Many breastfeeding moms (myself included) fall into the nurse-to-sleep trap. This starts out sweet and cute - you nurse your child until she falls into a peaceful sleep in your arms, and then you gently place her in the bassinet before crawling into bed yourself. Fast-forward to the four-month sleep regression, and you are now performing Olympic acts trying to keep your nipple in her mouth while you try to transfer her to her crib without waking her up. Good luck with that.

Now, please don't get me wrong. Breastfeeding had its beautiful moments for me, too. I just didn't always feel the good outweighed the bad.

What's that, you ask? Would I breastfeed again if we ever work up the courage to have another?

Absolutely.

It's the only way I'll ever fit into a size six pair of jeans again.

Dani Ryan grew up in South East Asia and landed a part as a hooker in a Chinese soap opera when she was only 13. Sadly, that was the end of her acting career. Three years ago, she quit her job as an executive at a large insurance company so she could stay home with her beautiful daughter. She now spends her days reading Sandra Boynton books, acting as a short-order cook, and trying to guess what time her husband will make it home for dinner. In her spare time, she writes about parenting and general nothingness on her humor blog, <u>Cloudy, With a Chance of Wine</u>.

Because I'm the Vagina Boss, That's Why
by Brenna Jennings
Suburban Snapshots

When I found out I was pregnant – somewhere between peeling myself off the floor under my bathroom sink and shoving a still-dripping pee stick between my husband's nose and his coffee – I knew I really wanted a girl. Of course health trumps genitalia, but I trusted that a fetus with the ability to plant itself in my business despite my intention to forever remain strictly an aunt was going to turn out just fine.

My sister was in the delivery room and saw the baby first, the umbilical cord was strategically placed and I remember the dragging seconds between her announcement of, "It's a . . . " and "girl!" She dropped my numb right leg and took the first gory pictures of my slimy daughter. My cousin took a keepsake photo of the placenta and let's all be grateful she didn't yet have a Facebook account.

It started off pretty typically at first, my husband wasn't exactly enthused about having to gingerly wipe between all those little girl creases and folds, but he maintained. He put on his game face and transitioned pretty smoothly from his former perspective to his new reality in which vaginas were strictly poop-collectors and frankly, kind of a chore.

See, no one tells you specifically that when you become the boss of a new human, you also become the COO of their reproductive organs. And because I was the only other non-canine female in the house, the bulk of responsibility fell to me.

"My vagina itches!" – *Go tell your mother.*

"It burns when I pee!" – *Go tell your mother.*

"When you wipe me it tickles!" – *I'm never changing you again. Go get your mother.*

At almost five, our daughter is all about her privates; she has theme songs, dances, she has underwear preferences and irritation issues, and most exciting to her, she has the word "vagina" and she will not hesitate to use it.

So my husband exists somewhere between addressing his daughter's needs and deferring to a more qualified authority; enjoying her creativity with lyrics and explaining that the whole express checkout line doesn't need to hear the Vagina Song, encouraging her independence and getting her to just put on the damned underpants and deal with the scratchy cotton crotch so we can leave the house today.

He's doing the best he can with his layman's understanding, and I respect his comfort level and efforts.

But God help us all when she hits puberty.

Brenna is a mom to one daughter and three dogs, works full-time, and writes her blog, <u>Suburban Snapshots</u>, in the evening to avoid having to read Dr. Seuss books at bedtime.

Wanted
by Kim Forde
The Fordeville Diaries

I'm not a celebrity, but I sometimes play one in my own mind.

Not because I want to attend red carpet events.

Not because I want to exist strictly on kale and coconut water.

No. I just want a personal assistant.

What's that you say? I don't need one?

OK, that's fair. If you want to get technical. I don't *need* one -- the way I *need*, say, an epidural very early in my upcoming childbirth process (I'm thinking around my 8th month).

I'm just saying that focusing more on my kids and less on my to-do list seems like a much better gig. Wouldn't it be nice to have someone take on all of the non-parenting household crap and make Operation Domestication hum like a well-oiled machine?

So just indulge me for a minute. It has been a long week. (Wait, it's Monday? WTF?)

* * *

WANTED: Personal Assistant for a busy mom flirting with insanity. Must be anal retentive, list-oriented and anticipatory. Mind reading helpful.

Key Responsibilities

- Serve as point person for daily interaction with contractors, repairmen and prospective vendors on various improvement and renovation projects for 100 year-old house. Conduct related due diligence and present findings/recommendations to employer. Alternatively, find employer new house.

- Pay household bills in timely fashion and assemble report of spending trends as they relate to family budget. Carve out employer's weekly Starbucks allowance. Liaise with financial planner to ensure employer's husband can, in fact, retire in this lifetime.

- Resolve ongoing showdown with public library on behalf of employer. Utilize stellar negotiation skills to remove proposed lifetime ban of family by producing at least 80% of overdue books.

- Handle all incoming mail management. Purge family name from unwanted lists -- repeatedly -- and discard all junk mail to avoid recycling pile that can be seen from space.

- Run various errands, including but not limited to: Dry cleaning, grocery shopping, filling prescriptions, library book returns (see above) and various returns of clothing items that don't look nearly as good in person as they did online. (Potential for increased year-end bonus if able to execute all returns within prohibitive 30-60 day windows.)

- Oversee all DVR management for household, ensuring that kids' programming never exceeds 65% of allowable storage. (Immediate termination may occur if employer's favorite shows are deleted.)

- Provide support as needed for all annual Christmas prep, including kick-ass cookie exchange baking, nightly placement of Elf on the Shelf and trips to Toys R Us as needed.

- Schedule, cancel and reschedule various family medical appointments as needed. Refrain from telling receptionist to remove the stick from her sizable ass.

- Research and determine, once and for all, the key differences between the 68 settings on employer's new dryer.

- Serve as Back-Up Reader for employer's monthly book club assignment, providing necessary plot point information as needed, in the probable event that employer does not surpass second chapter.

- Undertake all outstanding home furnishing needs in consultation with employer to replace current minimalist Target catalog look with that of an actual lived-in house. This includes procuring window treatments that cost less than a mortgage so employer's family may cease Family Fishbowl lifestyle in full view of neighborhood.

- Strategically participate, as appropriate, in any neighborhood gossip sessions and report back full list of names with corresponding house numbers to employer.

- Stay abreast of any emerging research on the possibility of intravenous caffeine products approved for residential use.

- Advise employer of any and all available, affordable maternity wear that does not resemble the following: Breaking Amish Mother-to-Be Collection, Muumuu Revival Trend or Anything Kardashian-esque.

- Present various family vacation options to employer after thorough research and site visits. Act as sole point person for all Disney World planning logistics, securing all meals and character meetings in advance.

- Ensure that the red and white wine household reserves are kept at an appropriately stocked level at all times. Maintain emergency reserve for natural disasters and school closures.

- Sustain employer's real-life friendships (non-Facebook, blog or Twitter) by scheduling monthly girls' night out or related activity to preserve employer's sanity. Also, coordinate occasional babysitters so employer and spouse may have a civilized meal out of the house and away from all sippy cups.

- Conduct any and all household interaction with the New Jersey DMV. No exceptions.

Necessary Qualifications

Must have experience dealing with the following:

- A well-meaning Type A employer who has the unpredictability of pregnancy hormones raging through her system.

- Employer's husband: All-around great guy -- with the exception of his propensity for bringing unauthorized Entenmann's products into household.

- Two children under age the age of six, who alternatively pretend to be ninjas, pirates and Disney royalty.

- Ornery middle-aged snoring pug who frequently appeals denied requests for bacon.

Additional Helpful Skills

- Ability to type 180 words per minute on mobile devices.

- Attention to detail -- specifically in organizing 3,894 fragments of plastic toys on a thrice-daily basis.

- Knowledge of crock pots and blog design.

All qualified applicants will be contacted for an in-person interview as soon as humanly possible. Mostly likely to be held at the local Starbucks or cupcake store.

Kim Forde writes about the art of perfecting domestic failure on her blog, The Fordeville Diaries. After nearly two decades in Manhattan, she now is a secret suburban convert with residual urban road rage. She abandoned the corporate grind to be a full-time SAHM to her two young kids (with a third on the way), which has led to both her Starbucks addiction and a healthy fear of craft stores. In addition, she is a proud survivor of the longest home renovation in modern American history. Armed with a keyboard and an addiction to storytelling, she can also be found wasting time on Facebook and Twitter.

Grown Up Words in a Pint-Sized Mouth
By Tracy Winslow
Momaical

"Then my son says to my daughter 'I'm going to park my boat in your vagina!'" says my friend, hilariously recalling last night's bath time antics. "And she responds with 'I'm going to park this train next to your penis!'" I am laughing while internally cringing. I realize I am far too immature to raise children. But it was too late. I already had them. And they were bouncing on the trampoline with the Boat Dock and the Train Depot. Fuck. I mean, the two and the three year old can say words like "penis" and "vagina" but they make my 38-year-old self blush just hearing them???

Vocabulary is extremely important and you are strongly judged by your word choices. It can make people respect or disdain you within a sentence or two. I have always spoken to my girls as if they are adults since they were born. People scoffed when I had a one-sided discussion with my 2-month-old about the merits of second language acquisition. Now my girls have an enviable lexicon and don't even question when I inform them that their behavior is reprehensible and that should they continue to act like heathens they shall be punished accordingly. I feel it's much nicer than saying "Hey, fuckers. You're robbing me of my will to live and right now I'd like to stick a giant straw into a box of Franzia and drink until you're less fucking annoying. You might want to go to your rooms before I go all white trash on yo' ass." Which, is really what I'm thinking and my tongue is bleeding from the effort of restraint.

I struggle enough with trying not to swear around my children. I paint in four letter words; much like an artist dabbles in oils or watercolors. It is my art. I cannot say things like: "Well, cock-a-doodle-doo. You just emptied an entire garsh dingle hopping bottle of vegetable oil on my fleepin-floppin kitchen floor" when the moment warrants a "Holy Fucking Mother of God on a Mule." Clearly I have no problem cursing like a sailor. Actually, come to think of it, sailors say "Brandy, you're a fine girl. What a good wife you would be." which I would never say. I guess then, more like a redneck – with Tourette's – in a trash talking contest - at a NASCAR race. However, words like "puberty" and "anus" embarrass the motherfuck out of me. I can't use them in normal conversation. I resort to using words like "pee-pee to" describe everything in the nether regions.

My husband knows this is my kryptonite and *loves* to torture me. He teases me incessantly to get me to blush by calling me monikers such as Wienersaurus Rex, Scrotodendrum, and Meat Whistle. Which are far superior and much more creative than when my ex-boyfriend called me a "Trick Ass Skank Ass Ho." Or when my sister's ex called her a "Chicken Rat Bitch Slut." Actually, come to think of it, that is pretty creative.

I know that I should teach my children anatomically correct words like "penis" and "vagina" – but I am too weak. I get shy using words like this at my yearly gynecologist appointment. One time, my two-year-old spotted my nephew's winger-wanger as he unexpectedly hopped into the tub with her after we went to the beach. Having been the first wienerschnitzel all up in her mix, she said "Oh, look! He has a waggly tail!" Sure, I could have embraced this teachable moment; but did I? Not a Twinkie's chance at a fat farm. "Yup. Waggly tail. He sure does."

Many of my friends use all the anatomically correct words with their children; hence the "Parking the boat in your vagina" conversation between siblings. I respect and admire this *but cannot emulate.* I simply can't bring myself to use words like "vagina" and "penis" with my girls. I have given birth to the most embarrassing friends I have ever had. I do NOT need to give them ammunition.

A few examples of my abject humiliation:

- The time when my daughter ordered a "pink taco" very loudly at the restaurant.
- Or when my daughters had this conversation in the middle of my yearly pap smear:

  Five-year-old Lena: *Mommy! Why is she poking you in the pee pee?*
  Two-year-old Emmeline: *Hey! Stweaker! You nakey! Hahahahahahahahaha!!!!*
  Lena: *Mommy. Seriously. She is STABBING YOU IN THE PEE PEE. Do I have to do that at my back to school doctor's appointment?*
- How about the multiple occasions my two-year-old has opened the stall door in the public restroom to give color commentary to all the people waiting to use the facilities? *"My mommy just putted a 'fire cwacker' in her bunners."* And then walked out like Miss America with a bouquet of super-soaker Tampax (leaving the door wide open for the world to witness me with my 7 For All Mankinds around my ankles). She handed them out like parting gifts to a group of amused women while I gathered up what little was left of my dignity and washed it down the sink.

- Once I walked into my (now) four-year-old daughter's room. She was playing nicely with her one-year-old sister. They are playing "birdies" with a pair of stuffed Bobwhites that sing when you squeeze their stomachs:

Me: What are you ladies doing?
Lena: We are playing birdies! This one's mine. Her name is Tweeter Twat.
My husband yells from his office: Hey! That's mommy's nickname too!
Emmeline: Twat, twat, twat, twat.
Me: Dear Mother of God.

So, as you can see, teaching my children to use words like "vagina" and "penis" would just add kerosene to my already blazing fire of embarrassment. Potty humor reigns up on high in our house. I often hear my children laughing diabolically while chanting "Tinkle, tinkle, little star" and working the word "poop" into just about everything they can. Maybe when they're teenagers I will teach them the correct terminology. On second thought, probably not. The more likely scenario is that my wuss-ass self will wait for them to learn all that important shit in health class. Because my immature brain can handle "Mommy! Emmeline is fucking around with my stuff!" much more easily than "Mommy, Emmeline just kicked me in the vulva!"

Tracy Winslow is a SAHM trying not to raise a flock of assholes. Besides crafting cocktails with Zoloft, Tracy can be found cursing, crying into her coffee over her stretch marks, Ouija-boarding her deceased metabolism and blogging humorously about her children and life at <u>Momaical</u>.

Giving The Milk Away For Free
By Kerry Rossow
HouseTalkN

"While you are young and free of stretch marks, you should be naked as much as possible," Said no mother ever.

I wish my mother had told me this. I wish someone had told me not to squander away the years of non-cellulite. My mother was busy reminding me not to give the milk away for free.

Pshhh...

I am going to start telling every hot, young thing I see to get naked as often as legally possible.

When I see pictures of my 25-year-old, bikini clad self, I remember being so self-conscious of my body. I want to tell that girl to lighten the frick up and strut up and down the beach. If I had that body back, I would walk around naked, holding a sign, "Check this out!"

This thought went through my head while I was in labor with my first child. The midwife suggested overloading my senses to distract from the contractions. There I was, naked, sitting on a birthing ball, sucking on a lollypop, making noises akin to cat in heat, while my husband rubbed my back.

When I looked over my shoulder at my sweet husband, I caught a glimpse of his face before he could recover. He was staring at the ceiling with extreme concentration. I realized that he wasn't using the Lamaze breathing to keep me in rhythm, he was using it to distract himself from the visual horror that was in front of him.

I Just Want to Pee Alone

As if this visual wasn't enough, more visuals soon followed.

The vision of me pushing out 10-12 pound babies.

Visions of an aureola the size of Texas.

Visions of my breasts attached to a pump.

Visions of vomit in my once silky hair.

Visions of my ovals of shame on the front of my shirt…at church.

With each baby, my body took a beating. The varicose veins in my legs look like a snake pit, my stretch marks look like a road map, and my boobs went from a 34B to a 36Long.

Here is the kicker. I'm not self-conscious of my body anymore. Not only did this body house and push out those babies but it also provides endless entertainment.

My pals and I yuk it up and show each other our battle scars with pride. "I'll see you your stretch marks and raise you with my hemorrhoids."

My husband (wisely) says that he much prefers this free and wild version to my reserved 25-year-old self.

When I once peed myself on a run, I walked through the door and told my husband, "I just peed all over the sidewalk." As we laughed ourselves silly, I knew that my 25-year-old self would have been mortified. My 35-year-old self couldn't wait to tell my bladder impaired friends.

But still, I wish that I had enjoyed that body more. I wish that I had known how fleeting it would be. I wish that I had known that the years of my body belonging to only me would not last forever. I wish that I could have enjoyed those years as much as I have enjoyed the years of my body being a baby factory, a milk buffet, a whoopee cushion, and the soft spot to fall.

For once, I wish that I hadn't listened to my mother. She was right about a lot of things- my big hair did look stupid, blue eye shadow was a mistake and the boy on the motorcycle was trouble. But, I should have given the milk away for free a lot more.

Kerry is a recovering teacher who blogs at <u>HouseTalkN</u>. Kerry blogs about house crashing, house stalking, and general life shenanigans. Her mother threatens to read that blog so she writes about things like 69 and her moral shortcomings at In The Powder Room. Kerry likes to talk about herself in the third person. Kerry would love to connect with you on Facebook and Twitter!

And Then There was That Time a Priest Called Me a Terrible Mother
By JD Bailey
Honest Mom

Ah, Mother's Day. That one day of the year that's supposed to be all about you, and then somehow isn't.

Or, if you're me, the day that *is* all about you, but not in the way you imagined. At all.

One Mother's Day, Hubs convinced me it would be a great idea to go to church before brunch. Now, I thought going to brunch with our baby and preschooler was pushing it. Church, too? I found that way overambitious.

But I went with it. Because, you know, Mother's Day is all about what Hubs wants.

So I loaded up the diaper bag with the bare necessities: Diapers. Wipes. Toys. Change of clothes for the baby. Diaper cream. Powder. Snacks. Books. Change of clothes for the three-year-old. Food for the kids at brunch. Hand sanitizer. Changing pad. Nursing cover. More snacks.

I got the preschooler ready. We fought over tights. Shoes. Dresses. Hair clips. Finally I gave up and let her wear a summer dress with tights and boots. Whatever. She was clothed.

I got the baby ready. Naturally, once she was dressed, she pooped on me. Then when she was re-dressed, she spit up. Finally she was clothed, fed, and relatively clean.

And then I had 12 minutes to get myself ready.

176

Honest Mom

Off we went to church, me with partially-dried hair and wearing my May Dress for church. When you go to church as infrequently as we do, one dress per month works. Score one for heathenism!

We grabbed our receipt for attending Mass (the bulletin, for you non-Catholics) and got settled in an inconspicuous pew off to the side. Hubs held Annie so she could see the singing and I breathed a sigh of relief that Grace passed out in her baby carseat.

I lip-synced with the opening hymn with the rest of the parishioners, certain the noise would wake up Grace. But she stayed asleep.

When my kids remained quiet through the first part of Mass, I thought maybe miracles do occur after all. This was actually, kind of, a little bit . . . peaceful!

But then we got to the homily. And all hell broke loose.

The kids? Oh, no, they were fine.

It was me who lost her shit.

We watched the very old and very white priest hobble up to the pulpit. I was expecting to hear some quaint little sermon about his darling deceased Irish mother, bless her soul.

The priest started his sermon benignly enough. Mothers are lovely, they give us life, blah, blah, blah. But then it took an unexpected turn.

I sat there in disbelief as I was told that women should be home with their children, where they belong.

I started twitching when the priest lectured that mothers who worked could not possibly be good mothers when they actually *were* home because the workplace was too stressful.

And I think I may have cut off Hubs' circulation while gripping his arm as the priest concluded that the competition of the work-place made women lose their feminine qualities and turned them into bitches. Naturally, the priest surmised, as I turned beet red, no child deserved THAT.

(And I don't remember that the priest said "bitches," but Hubs swears that he did.)

I think what happened next was that Hubs physically restrained me from leaping over the pews to strangle that old bastard. But I'm not totally sure. I was a teeny bit verklempt.

I sat there and seethed. I plotted the priest's demise. I cursed Hubs for his bright idea to go to church that morning.

I finally stole a glance at Hubs, who had the good sense to look as horrified as I did. I wanted to leave. I think he did too. But the baby was still sleeping and Anne was happily listening to the music.

So I put the kids' contentment ahead of my desire to make a scene and stomp out of there. BECAUSE I AM A GOOD MOTHER, DAMMIT.

Instead, I spent the rest of the service having conversations in my head with that priest that went something like this:

Crotchety Old Priest: Women belong in the home.

Me: Fuck you.

Crotchety Old Priest: Women who work can't be good mothers.

Me: Screw off.

Crotchety Old Priest: Working makes women unfeminine.

Me: You're a dumbass.

I'm nothing if not mature.

When it seemed like an acceptable time to bolt, we did. And in the safety of a nearby restaurant, after nursing my baby and cutting up my preschooler's food, I guzzled my mimosa and chowed down my cold waffles.

It was Mother's Day. I had spent the entire day putting everyone else's needs before mine. And I had sat and listened as I was insulted by an old man who told me I was a terrible mother because I worked.

Mother's Day was supposed to be a day where I was treated like a queen. Even at church. *Especially* at church. Church of the Holy Blessed Mother, my ass.

Where was my sermon that thanked me for my selflessness, extolled my beauty, and praised my amazing ability to diaper with one hand and put a dress on a princess doll with another while paying bills over the phone and cuddling a toddler?

Instead, I had been shit on. Literally and figuratively.

So I did what any other unfeminine, bitchy, working mother would do. I ordered another mimosa—hold the OJ. I watched my children make a mess and husband try to control the chaos. And sipped my drink while I looked forward to abandoning my family in the afternoon to get my nails done.

I was already damned, right? Might as well enjoy it while I could.

I Just Want to Pee Alone

JD Bailey blogs at <u>Honest Mom</u>, where she writes about raising her young daughters and managing her ongoing depression. With real candor and a good dose of humor, JD writes to maintain her sanity and connect with other moms. She loves her family, her wine, and her Mac-Book, and is not a fan of working out, bad coffee, or people with no concept of personal space. Which means her kids might be in trouble, considering they are always thisclose to her.

It's Not a Toomah
by Jen
People I Want to Punch in the Throat

In the fall of 2004, I was working full time as a Realtor. Over the last two years, I had built a successful real estate career and I was really starting to enjoy my life. The Hubs and I had been married for a couple of years and we still hadn't worked kids into the life plan at that point. We knew we wanted some, but down the road. Way down the road.

That fall I started experiencing some unusual symptoms. It started with the ridiculously tender boobs. I've always had enormous knockers, but suddenly they started growing like mutant append-ages. I was busting out of bras that had fit me for years. I was pop-ping buttons on shirts that normally had no problem staying closed.

One morning I was working out with my mother and I started complaining about how sore my breasts were. My mother stopped her elliptical machine and stared at me with a mixture of joy and loathing. Joy because she was positive I was pregnant and might give her another grandchild and loathing because she was posit-ive I was pregnant and she couldn't believe how stupid I was. "Are you pregnant?" she asked tentatively, as if I might miscarry right there from the shock.

"God, no!" I said hastily.

"Are you sure? Are you guys . . ." my mother said. "Is everything . . . working . . ." she tried again.

"Mother," I hissed. "Everything is fine! I can't be pregnant! I am on the Pill!" She should know. She's the one who put me on the Pill when I was 12 because I had horrific and irregular periods.

"Well, when was the last time you had your period?" she asked.

"I don't know," I said. "I only get them a few times a year now and I always forget when the last time was."

I started to think. When was the last time I bought tampons? Yikes, it *had* been a while. But I couldn't be pregnant. I was on the Pill!

A few weeks later I strapped my huge hooters into a new giant bra and headed out to show houses to a new client. It was early evening and I was literally falling asleep at the wheel. "John," I said. "I'm so tired tonight. You need to talk to me and help me stay awake or else we're going to end up in the ditch!"

John was a bit nervous, and then he was downright freaked out when I threw up in the bushes of the next house we visited. "What the hell?!" he exclaimed when he saw me duck around the side of the house so I could vomit in private.

"Sorry. I couldn't help it. It just came over me," I said, shaken. Ever the professional, I popped a piece of gum in my mouth and unlocked the door.

That night I received an email from John:

Jen, I was thinking about your symptoms [he did not know about my tender boobies] *and I did some research. I think you should see a doctor right away. I think you could have pancreatic cancer. Sorry. And good luck. I could be totally wrong. Are you available tomorrow at 5 so we can see that house again where you puked?*

Cancer? I hadn't even thought of cancer. Since I was so positive I wasn't pregnant, I naturally assumed it was cancer and started planning my funeral. It was going to be beautiful. I wanted every-one to share a funny story about how I touched their lives and made it better. I wanted doves released at the end of the service as a sign of hope and new beginnings. Oh, and I wanted to be cremated and have my ashes sprinkled in the yards of all my loved ones with just a scoop of me saved for Hubs to keep on his mantle for all time.

The Hubs was still young enough to find another wife. He could move back to New York and forget me (except for the bit of me on his mantle, of course). He'd be sad for awhile, but imagine how many women he could land with his tragic tale of losing his be-loved and beautiful wife in the prime of her life? He'd be hotter than he'd ever been. My premature death would be the best thing that ever happened to his sex life.

Yup, I was pretty sure I had cancer. *Or maybe you're pregnant, dummy,* a voice inside my head said. Nope. This was my own *Love Story.* I was dying. *I'm pretty sure you're pregnant, you moron,* the voice said again. I attributed the voices to the cancer moving into my brain.

Finally, when I couldn't ignore my symptoms any longer (or plan a more beautiful funeral) I told the Hubs late one night while we laid in bed, "Hubs. I have something to tell you," I whispered.

"What's up?" he asked.

"Well, you know how I haven't been feeling well for the past couple of weeks?"

"Yeah."

"Well, my client, John. Do you remember me talking about him? Four bedrooms, 3 baths, 3 car garage big enough to park his boat in and a finished basement for a pool table?"

"Yeah, I know him. He also wants a big yard for his dog, right?"

"Yes, preferably fenced, but that's not a deal breaker. Anyway. John did some research and he thinks I have cancer . . . or I might be pregnant."

The Hubs was silent for a full minute.

"Is John a doctor?" he finally asked.

"No. He's an engineer," I replied.

The Hubs was silent for another full minute.

"You're kind of wishing for cancer!" I accused him.

"I wouldn't say 'wishing'," he replied. "I'm just thinking that cancer might be a hell of a lot easier to deal with than a baby. I mean look at us. We're not fit to be parents. You've been 'sick' for 12 weeks now and all we've done is ignored it and hope it goes away. You don't have cancer, Jen. You're pregnant and we've been too stupid and lazy and irresponsible to even deal with that. How will we take care of a baby? No. We'd better hope it's cancer."

The next morning I peed on 10 sticks and all 10 confirmed that I did not have cancer.

People I Want to Punch in the Throat

Jen is the anonymous blogger throwing hilarious punches peppered with a liberal dose of f-bombs on her blog <u>*People I Want to Punch in the Throat*</u>*. Jen is also the author of* Spending the Holidays with People I Want to Punch in the Throat. *She has been featured on* The Huffington Post, *Babble, and* Headline News.

The various awards that she's received include such keepers as BlogHer 2012 Voice of the Year, Circle of Moms Top 25 Funniest Mom Blogs 2012 and 2013, Circle of Moms Top 25 Book Author Moms, and Cutest Blog Award (this one was sent to her accidentally and has since been rescinded, since her blog looks like shit).

She is wife to The Hubs and mother to Gomer and Adolpha (not their real names – their real names are actually so much worse).

Made in the USA
San Bernardino, CA
09 November 2017